WHERE THE LIGHT LIVES

Advance praise for *Where The Light Lives*

"*Where The Light Lives* is a beautifully written account of a young woman's extraordinary visionary experiences. Diagnosed with a painful and humiliating disease of the spine, Linda Cull wanted to die. Without even nearly dying, she then had a series of encounters with a dazzling light-being that transformed her life. Similar to the classic near-death experience, Linda's sense of being flooded with lessons from a transcendent source awakened her artistic imagination, which launched her on a career as a brilliant painter. Her book is a document of hope to all and should expand the horizons of human psychology."

Michael Grosso, PhD,
author of *Experiencing The Next World Now*

"… a delightful story of a woman who has had a remarkable journey through the psychic-sphere where spiritually transformative experiences are a way of life for her. Along the way, the paranormal becomes normal and she is able to walk between the worlds melding this life with the other, heavenly side. This is a book you will want to read!"

Jody Long, author of *God's Fingerprints:*
Impressions of Near-Death Experiences

"… an open-hearted, intimate and very personal account about the content and after-effects of the many spiritually transformative experiences by the author. The reader needs an open mind to really understand and to empathise with the impact of these overwhelming conscious experiences."

**Pim van Lommel, cardiologist,
author of *Consciousness Beyond Life:
The Science of the Near-Death Experience***

"Where *The Light Lives* is a reminder that spiritually transcendent experiences offer us a myriad of ways to access the eternal. They teach us that we are to bring those eternal truths to bear upon our daily world. Linda Cull has filled her book with her own personal stories that will amaze readers."

Nancy Clark, author of *Divine Moments: Ordinary People Having Spiritually Transformative Experiences*

"Journeying into the Light with Linda is the closest you can get to heaven while you are still breathing."

**Anthony Grzelka, author of *Life and Beyond: A Medium's
Guide to Dealing with
Loss and Making Contact***

"Down-to-earth accessible, Linda's story is full of light, hope and hard-won wisdom – a story for the soul."

**Frith Luton, author of *Bees, Honey and the Hive:
Circumambulating the Centre
(A Jungian Exploration of the
Symbolism and Psychology)***

WHERE THE LIGHT LIVES

A TRUE STORY
ABOUT DEATH, GRIEF
AND TRANSFORMATION

LINDA CULL

FOREWORD BY DR PENNY SARTORI

WILARA PRESS

The names of some individuals in this book have been changed to protect their privacy.

First published in 2015 by Wilara Press
PO Box 360
Inglewood, WA, Australia, 6932

Copyright © Linda Cull 2015

The moral right of the author has been asserted.

All rights reserved. No part of this book may be reproduced or transmitted by any person or entity, including internet search engines or retailers, in any form or by any means, electronic or mechanical, including photocopying (except under the statutory exceptions provisions of the Australian Copyright Act 1968), recording, scanning or by any information storage and retrieval system, without prior permission in writing from the publisher.
This book is not intended as a substitute for the medical advice of physicians. You should consult a physician in matters relating to your health and particularly with respect to any symptoms that may require diagnosis or medical attention. In the event you use any of the information in this book for yourself, the author and the publisher assume no responsibility for your actions.

National Library of Australia Cataloguing-in-Publication entry
    Cull, Linda, author.

    Where the light lives : a true story about death, grief and transformation / Linda Cull ;
    Dr Penny Sartori, foreword ; Frith Luton, editor.

    ISBN: 9780994359308 (paperback)
    ISBN: 9780994359315 (ebook)

    Cull, Linda.
    Near-death experiences.
    Experience (Religion). Spiritual life.
    Spiritual healing. Self-consciousness (Awareness)--Religious aspects. Self-actualization (Psychology)--Religious aspects. Spiritual biography--Australia.

    204.092

Cover and internal design by Damonza
Printed by Ingram/Lightning Source in the United States of America, United Kingdom and Australia.

For Robert & our darling boys, Oliver & Daniel, with love
And in loving memory of my ancestors & dear Aunty May

"We are all visitors to this time, this place. We are just passing through. Our purpose here is to observe, to learn, to grow, to love… and then we return home."

— AUSTRALIAN ABORIGINAL PROVERB

Table of Contents

Foreword xiii
Introduction. xvii
Prologue: Journey Home. 1
One: Death & Suffering 3
Two: Calling My Name. 11
Three: Challenges. 23
Four: Ultimate Power Reality 31
Five: Life Review & Preview 39
Six: Synchronicity. 47
Seven: Psychic Development. 55
Eight: Inspired Creativity 61
Nine: African Woman. 67
Ten: Master Teacher 73
Eleven: Out-of-Body. 81
Twelve: Deaconess After-Death. 91
Thirteen: May Transitioning 101
Fourteen: Signs of Survival 109
Fifteen: Revelations. 117
Sixteen: Divine Illuminations 125

Seventeen: Medium 133
Eighteen: Power of Thought 143
Nineteen: Hallucinations & Delusions 153
Twenty: Premonitions............................. 161
Epilogue... 169
Acknowledgements............................... 173
About the Author................................ 177

Foreword

SPIRITUALLY TRANSFORMATIVE EXPERIENCES (STEs) are fascinating experiences. They first grabbed my attention over twenty years ago and I have studied them in depth ever since. They are not new but have played a role in human experience throughout history and can occur in many contexts. Some STEs occur quite unexpectedly and spontaneously, whereas others follow a period of deep introspection, personal crisis, illness, intense spiritual practice or a close brush with death (near-death experience).

Many organisations have dedicated years of study to such experiences. The Alister Hardy Society for the Study of Spiritual Experience was founded in 1969 at Manchester College Oxford, England, by biologist Sir Alister Hardy. The University of Wales, Lampeter currently houses the society's archive of over 6000 reported cases. In more recent years there has also been the launch of the American Center for the Integration of Spiritually Transformative Experiences.

Despite there being an increasing number of reports, STEs have not been taken seriously or considered in depth by most people except by those who have experienced or decided to study them. The general public mostly takes them at surface value and dismisses them as hallucinations. This, in turn, deters the public sharing of such an experience, resulting in experiencers feeling isolated and left struggling to understand these overwhelming experiences. So the general public remain mostly misinformed and unaware of the full extent of these deeply empowering and transformative experiences.

Where the Light Lives is an insightful book describing the STEs of Linda Cull. It begins with a description of Linda's interesting family history and cultural background and of how her life was as a young girl. There is a marked contrast between her family's experience of living through war and then their life after emigration from Croatia to Australia. It highlights well how the effects of war can still impact on later generations.

For Linda, a diagnosis of acute idiopathic scoliosis at the age of fourteen and the response of her peers contributed to feelings of humiliation, stress and sadness. She often felt alone and, at times, even suicidal. She frequently asked God for help, often praying for a miracle.

Then from the young age of sixteen years, Linda began having spiritual experiences which she initially did not understand and put to the back of her mind. It was only when they became more prevalent and impacting, along with other synchronicities in her life, that Linda began to take notice of them. When she learned to trust these synchronicities and experiences they had a beneficial effect, for her and in many cases for others. Gradually the experiences increased in frequency and, when Linda was in her twenties, they became a very common occurrence.

It was particularly perturbing to read about what happened when Linda sought help in understanding her experiences. Like many others who have undergone similar experiences, she met with much frustration. She describes confiding in a priest whose response left her feeling humiliated and disappointed. She sought further help from medical professionals but Linda's description of how her experiences were perceived by the medical community is a reflection of how poorly understood these important experiences are within today's society.

With greater awareness of STEs gained through books like this, more people will realise that they are not alone in having spiritual experiences and it will encourage them also to share their experiences. More importantly, it will inform people, who know little about STEs, of the full range of complexities associated with them. Linda's story is beautifully written and of great healing benefit. It will be a great source of comfort to many people.

Penny Sartori, PhD,
author of *The Wisdom of Near-Death Experiences*

Introduction

I WROTE THIS book hoping to enrich the lives of others and to give hope to many. During life *you* will be transformed by your experiences and sometimes in remarkable ways. And some of these experiences will have such an impact, that they will reverberate for many years to come and affect the lives of others. Such has been my experience having encountered the higher-power a number of times – this awesome force reverberates throughout my life and may now stir your imaginings for what is possible.

In sharing my account of spiritual illumination and healing from deep psychological pain I hope that you will remember your Divine connection and feel encouraged to foster an awareness of God or Spirit in your daily life. There is no right way to God/Spirit, only your way. What may appear to be the 'wrong' way by other people's standards may indeed be the perfectly inspired path by which you will arrive at clarity of mind and a more authentic expression of yourself.

For more than twenty years I have either experienced extraordinary states of consciousness or have been dealing with integrating these into my daily life. At the age of sixteen, I had my first of many out-of-body experiences (OBEs) – at twenty-one, my first of many 'light' experiences where I encountered the higher-power and was forever changed by it – at twenty-two, a panoramic life review and preview... in heaven.

In the spiritual realm I have met magical beings imparting love and wisdom, and experienced many other elements typically associated with a phenomenon commonly known as the *near-death experience (NDE)*.

Researchers have classified the NDE phenomenon differently – Moody, Ring, Sabom, Greyson and others. Amongst them, however, the general consensus is that a near-death experiencer will have experienced one, some or more of the following: a sense of their consciousness separating from their body – the out-of-body experience, in the OBE state they are able to observe their physical body and environment; a sense of freedom; the absence of pain; intense emotions – often rapture and unconditional love; rapid movement – perhaps through a 'tunnel'; an encounter with a powerful being of light; encounters with deceased relatives, religious figures, spiritual guardians, heavenly environments, a panoramic life review/preview and a barrier of some kind that inhibits them from remaining in the spiritual realm.

Notably, a NDE is ineffable. The experiencer often struggles to verbalise the profound spiritual event and is often reluctant to share it for fear of having their experience invalidated by another's scepticism. Tellingly, the experiencer is altered by their NDE – sometimes profoundly.

By my early thirties, I had heard of the term near-death experience but never paid it particular attention. I didn't think it was relevant to me. As the term suggests, I assumed a person had to be 'near-death', in the physical sense, to experience it and I never had been.

It wasn't until my eldest son was two and a-half and I was thirty-four, when we visited our local library together that I noticed a book on a shelf whose title made mention of being 'transformed by the light'. I immediately thought – *I've been transformed by the light*.

I began to browse through the book with interest and then viewed a list of characteristics which typically define the phenomenon and remarkably, I had experienced many of these. This, for me, was a revelation. I suddenly realised that the NDE was very pertinent to me.

It was a great relief to finally know that there was a term for the kinds of spiritual occurrences I had experienced and I felt validated by this. My experiences didn't just live in my imagination, but were other people's personal experiences too. From that time on, I could neatly sum up the remarkable in my life, as I never could before. Therefore, it is also my hope that this book will inspire a similar feeling of clarity and acceptance in other experiencers.

The following chapters detail my transcendent experiences and my healing journey from depression and intergenerational grief to contentment and wellbeing. They describe what it is like to go beyond the physical body and to enter into expansive states of consciousness. And they explain the various after-effects that can ripple throughout daily life following encounters with the powers of heaven. I invite you to find in my words an example on how to embrace and nurture your personal spirituality.

PROLOGUE
JOURNEY HOME

"OH, THERE'S THE Light again!" I rejoiced, transfixed by the astonishingly beautiful luminosity before me. My great longing for The Light and The Light's great longing for me propelled my spirit forwards through the tunnel.

All the qualities I had experienced of The Light before – the power, magnetism, unconditional love and acceptance – emanated from The Light at the end of this long spiritual pipeline. At the end of this tunnel was home; it was heaven and I knew this implicitly. I was rejoicing in my homecoming and The Light was rejoicing in it too.

My next journey to heaven was something similar – I felt myself soaring like a bird. I was overjoyed to be out-of-body again, totally liberated from the flesh. I knew where my body was but felt no attachment to it. It was in bed, asleep on earth, yet the spiritual me was wide awake. I felt every bit like myself, though expanded.

I knew my route 'home' instinctively. I had flown it many, many times. Home was not on earth but in heaven. I was so attracted to The Light I saw ahead of me that I flew towards it at an unthinkable speed. My entire being anticipated the bliss of my homecoming.

As much as I desired to touch it, The Light also reached out to me, eager for the ultimate cosmic embrace. Then, as I drew nearer to the entrance of heaven, I became aware of the tunnel's 'membrane'. The Light of heaven was shining upon it.

I observed how the 'walls' of the tunnel throbbed with incessant movement like waves out at deep sea. I felt I was being birthed through this channel into another world.

ONE
DEATH & SUFFERING

I WAS BORN AND raised in an island paradise on the opposite side of the world to the mountains and valleys of my ancestors. In Australia, I always felt abundant, fortunate and free. My earliest memory of life is that of sitting in a warm lilac bathtub full of bubbles up to my ears – I felt very happy.

As a child, I spent endless days playing with my older sister Mary and our young neighbours in an idyllic suburban setting. Our street was abuzz with activity. We roamed and we had enviable freedoms.

Death entered my awareness at an early age because my immigrant parents slaughtered animals in our backyard in Perth. It was the late 1970s and little could I grasp then that death and its meaning would become a central feature of my life – spurred on by numerous spiritual experiences in my teens, twenties and thirties.

I recall as a little girl, squatting by my mum's side and watching her slit the necks of chickens along the periphery of her much admired rose garden. The blood trickling out of the birds would pool and then drain into the dirt. The bright red blood was a similar colour to the bulbous flowers overhead that dropped one or two fragrant petals, in a display of pity for the birds.

Too young to ponder the finality of life, I rather marvelled at how these creatures could run about without their heads on. I laughed and, yet, was equally afraid at the sight of them. Once they'd exhausted themselves, mum took the headless chooks into the house for plucking.

She plucked their feathers in the deep laundry sink. I didn't stay there at her side for long as the stink was thick and overpowering. The laundry window fogged up with steam rising from the boiling hot water mum poured from a kettle, over the chickens. As she laboured, her face gleamed with beads of sweat and her expression was such that it appeared she gained absolutely no pleasure from the task at hand.

I began to believe that death was a rather solemn and final-curtain event when I was five and my paternal grandmother died. My dad arrived home from work one afternoon and my mum handed him a white envelope that he then took to their bedroom. My mum told me to leave him well alone but I was wildly intrigued by all the mystery surrounding that envelope.

A few moments later, I quietly peered around the doorway of my parent's bedroom and saw my dad sitting on his side of the bed, crying. He was facing the wardrobe and, though his back was turned to me, I could see him wiping his face with a handkerchief. I felt very uncomfortable seeing my daddy crying. I understood he was looking at pictures of his dead mother because earlier that day I'd overheard mum speaking with a man who'd entered our home. He had returned from a holiday to my parent's homeland of Croatia (then Yugoslavia) and was delivering the photographs from dad's family.

Dad was very fond of his mother – he always spoke kindly of her caring nature and generosity. She'd had an awfully difficult life. During the Second World War, when food was scarce, she hid small pieces of dried bread in the pockets of her skirt especially for dad, her youngest child of seven – this was a treat.

I wanted to know, what exactly did a dead grandmother look like? I returned to the lounge room and waited there until dad had left his bedroom. I then took my chance to go in and rummage through his drawers. My parents were busy with tasks and didn't notice me. I crept quietly around my parent's bed and squatted by dad's bedside table. I opened the bottom drawer carefully to retrieve the white envelope, which my dad had placed there.

At one glance the drawer spoke volumes about my dad. It was meticulously clean and ordered; a habit he'd acquired from his army days. There were lots of papers and envelopes stacked together and everything had its rightful place. Even at the young age of five, I knew I had to pay particular attention to where the envelope belonged so I could return it there.

I discovered the envelope, thick with photos, beneath the passports. Opening it, I carefully pulled the photos out and held them in my little hand. There were perhaps six in total and I began to view the collection. Firstly I viewed pictures of the funeral procession – a man held the national flag and others carried rustic instruments. An old stone wall meandered through the country side with mourners walking by it, behind a coffin on the back of a cart pulled by a donkey. I recognised some of the people in the pictures as my extended family – they appeared bereaved. *My dead Baba must be in that box*, I thought.

I then came upon the most remarkable image of my young life and it made a startling impression upon me. It was a close up view of my dead grandmother – Baba Mara appeared to be asleep. I peered closely at her face. It looked like crumpled crepe paper and her hair was covered by a rose-coloured headscarf.

Baba Mara was a traditional woman who, when alive, to express her grief, at the loss of her husband and son, wore mournful black clothes with a scarf to match that covered her thinning hair. In death, however, she wore colour. It was the first occasion

I'd ever seen her looking so bright and, though she looked old and still, she also looked happier than I'd ever seen her look before.

I snuck into my parent's bedroom to look at the photographs of my dead grandmother many times. I always sought the same picture from the envelope – the one of the open casket – and I was never found out. In bed with the light off, I sometimes wondered what my death would be like. I imagined my own son grieving my earthly departure and I cried myself to sleep.

At seven years of age – the same age at which my dad had lost his father – the theme of death continued to weave its way through my consciousness when my dad died on the operating table. It was during open-heart surgery, when he experienced cardiac arrest and his heartbeat flat-lined for more than two minutes. He was, however, brought back to life with the use of defibrillators. What I vaguely understood then was that my dad's illness stemmed from a bout of rheumatic fever that he developed as a child. However this was not the complete story, and it wasn't until I was an adult that I learnt he has a connective tissue disorder called Marfan syndrome that contributed to his poor health.

Dad was diagnosed with Marfan syndrome by his doctors. They suggested that this condition and having rheumatic fever as a child, when he became very ill from sleeping in cold, damp caves during the war, meant that he had developed a weakened heart valve. This malfunctioning valve was then replaced with a new valve when he was forty-six years of age.

Visiting dad at the Royal Perth Hospital following his surgery was a secret anxiety-filled mission. Children were not allowed in the intensive care unit but a caring nurse smuggled my sister and me in because dad had become depressed and she believed seeing us would lift his spirits. I recall my dad crying at the sight of us, and him being connected to seemingly countless tubes and machines. My mum believed my dad might die again and this was perhaps the last time he would ever see his girls.

Though I was quite young at the time, I was aware of the seriousness of his condition and the stress my mum was experiencing. I recognised in my dad a vulnerable man, and from then on, all of life became vulnerable and unpredictable. Dad made it through intensive care and returned home, though his physical and psychological health, and the potential of his demise hung over our family life impacting our emotional lives for many years to come. Dad suffered from bouts of anxiety about his health but he also carried on with his sense of humour intact, often joking in his thick accent, "I die but nothing there – nothing! Dead mean dead. Kaput! Finito!" His new heart valve was derived from a pig and so he also delighted in telling anyone who'd listen, "I be part man, part pig!"

Following my grandmother's death and my dad's death and resurrection, I acquired a great compassion for the sheep that were being slaughtered in our backyard. One or two sheep were killed there or at a relative's backyard each Christmas and Easter and sometimes for other special occasions too. It was always a bittersweet occasion for me, when my merriment for the day's festivities was marred by the suffering of others.

Often, just before the slaughter, I'd muster up the courage to visit the sheep hoping to comfort it. The sheep always looked sad to see me. I would find it lying on the back lawn, on its side in the hot sun, with its legs tied together. For a child, it was a heartbreaking scene. All I ever wanted to do was to set the poor animal free but I never had the courage to do so. I was afraid of being reprimanded and, by all considerations, I knew the sheep wouldn't get very far should I have dared to free it.

Feeling sad and guilty, I'd run inside the house and hide in my bedroom until the slaughter was over. Even with my bedroom door shut I could still hear the back and forth motion of the butcher's knife as it was being sharpened. I'd push my fingers into my ears and hum, to block out the noise of my dad preparing for the kill. I prayed to God to help the doomed sheep, but that help never came.

Sometimes, I'd stand at the back door and peer through the flyscreen to watch the slaughter. It took two strong men to hold a sheep still, as it jerked for its freedom – usually my dad, his brother or their nephew – it was hard yakka, brow-sweating work. I could see the men bent over the animal between the slits of my fingers that covered my eyes. I heard their tense voices and the cry of the sheep to its death. Only when the dreaded commotion was over, and I was very sure that the sheep was completely dead, did I dare venture outside. By then, curiosity got the better of me and I proceeded cautiously across the back lawn and up the brick steps, leading to my dad's elevated vegetable patch. There I'd view the sheep's blood pooled in a hole from where, ordinarily, dad grew the choicest harvest each season.

The men, at this time, were with the lifeless creature on the lawn, skinning it. I then descended the steps to get a closer look at them working on the animal, fascinated by its anatomy. I'd think, *Without its wool on a sheep looks rather skinny and a bit silly*. Once skinned, the sheep was hung up by thick steel hooks from the clothesline, while laundry buckets held its organs. I liked to look at the liver and the kidneys – my parents ate these.

The stomach, digestive tract, heart and lungs were thrown into the hole in the vegetable garden, but sometimes before dad did this, he'd blow the lungs up like a balloon to show me how well they expanded. I thought it was a brilliant sight. Our Aussie neighbours, no doubt, considered us a bit strange for (amongst other things) hanging a dead sheep from the clothesline where ordinarily our garments dried.

Unfortunately for the poor animal, a lamb or sheep cooked on a spit tastes very good – and by the time it had been rotating over a fire for hours, its flesh browned, salted and made crispy, it appeared less of the creature it once was and more like a much-desired lunch. Our extended family then gathered around the dining room table with feelings of joy and gratitude for the meal provided.

In our family love was expressed readily through food. An abundance of food on my plate equated to an abundance of parental love. I should well have been the width of a bus because I was so full up on love.

It was not until I was a woman and dad had long stopped slaughtering sheep in the backyard, that he shared his true sentiments about it.

"It be very hard for me to kill the sheep," he said to me one day. "I happy I not have to do anymore."

"What do you mean, dad?" I asked, rather surprised by his remark.

"I really do not like killing creatures," he confessed.

His admission made me stop to consider – perhaps the men who had slaughtered our family members during the war, didn't like killing either.

TWO
CALLING MY NAME

I SAT ON THE floor and leant against a hard, cold wall to watch my mum getting ready for work. She always dressed immaculately.

The pain in me was so great I thought my heart might rupture. Mum looked into the mirror and applied bright lipstick to her lips.

"I wish I was dead," I uttered, the words clawing at my throat.

"Don't be silly, Linda," she scolded me, her brow furrowing.

I went quiet. I had failed to make her understand how depleted I was feeling. I felt I didn't have the stamina to go on anymore. I was ashamed of my inability to conquer the gloom pervading me and I felt more hopeless than ever before.

After this, I only ever uttered my words of grief to God.

A succession of profoundly healing heavenly miracles followed – altering the course of my life.

Teenagers are known for their complexities but my situation was more complex. The murder of my grandfather had produced more grief than I can utter – the kind that festers under the skin. I was born with grief in my DNA, though I was one generation removed from the source of profound suffering. Nonetheless it shaped my life.

I was born of two cultures but felt I belonged to neither. The first was a close-knit community of Croatian immigrants who were devastated by the Second World War. Many, like my parents, left the former Yugoslavia post-war as there were limited opportunities in their homeland. They sought a better life for their families and so relocated.

The challenges that confronted my father and mother, our extended family and traditional community, became superimposed upon my own life. I was therefore concerned by all the abuses and social injustices happening everywhere that I had ever heard about.

The second culture was that of my birthplace, Australia – then a nation well established according to English traditions, yet in the throes of extensive social change.

As a child I admired the strength, enterprise and generosity of my traditional people, who had survived great adversity, yet I yearned to belong to mainstream culture. I wanted to be like other 'typical' Aussie kids on the block – sun-browned, thong-wearing and carefree. So I rejected my parent's native tongue and I tried to blend in as best I could. But I frequently felt on the outer, not quite fitting the mould. My family was loud and emotional and we stood out in the line at the local shops!

I was christened, as a baby, in the Catholic faith and this was as much an expression of my parents' political liberation as it was a religious gesture. In their homeland, villagers had secretly defied authorities to have their children christened in the thick of night.

Mum, Mary and I attended church at Infant Jesus in Morley and I spent my time there reviewing disturbing images of the crucifixion and a very large statue of Jesus on the cross, with nails protruding from his hands and feet.

Mum believed Christianity fostered strong ethics in life and, though my parents were not strict Catholics, religion impacted our lives. Mum made me quite aware of God's watchful eye which caused me to fear His wrath. Mostly, I tried to do the 'right thing' by my Catholic God and Croatian mother, but there were regular lapses in my attention span and often enough I felt I'd let the 'big-man' down.

By contrast, my dad only ever entered a church if he felt he really had to – for christenings, weddings or funerals. Otherwise he flatly refused to go.

"God be everywhere," he'd chuckle.

His mistrust of priests ran deep – back to his wartime experiences when some men of God participated in unholy acts.

"He not getting my money!" He'd speak loudly, in his broken English, as the collection bag went around the congregation. "Why priest not get job like-a-me," he'd say louder, "Nobody give-a-me money for nothing!"

His sudden outburst would rebound off the cold church walls and into the ears of God.

Oh dear God, I'd pray, squirming in the pew. *Sorry Jesus, please forgive dad – don't send him to hell – he's been injured by war!*

"Stealing from the people!" My dad would exclaim, refusing to part with his coins.

We quickly dropped our loose change into the bag so as to conceal just how little we were actually giving and with one final quick gesture, my sister would thump him as a reprisal for his obvious lack of tact – causing mum further embarrassment and dad to roar with laughter.

For all his anti-church maverick behaviour, dad was a great believer in the power of prayer. Both our parents encouraged us to pray to a higher-power from an early age and it is this open dialogue with God that ultimately saved my life. Prayer was my lifeline when, as a teenager, life became very bleak for me.

At fourteen, I was diagnosed with adolescent idiopathic scoliosis

– a deformity of the spine. I had developed an abnormal side-to-side S-shaped curvature with a twist that pulled my ribs out of their natural alignment, causing me varying degrees of muscular and ligament pain. I was by then awkwardly thin and six-foot tall.

On the surface of daily life I functioned adequately enough. I had good friends. I laughed. I got good grades. I had dreams for the future. But in private moments I unravelled. In the late 1980s I attended a working-class high school where oddities of nature were openly ridiculed. Children teased me about my height and asked if my parents fed me enough, when in truth, I was overfed. The unwanted attention I ceaselessly attracted caused me considerable angst. Daily bouts of mortification eroded my self-esteem and I became very self-conscious about my appearance. At home, I took to measuring myself, rather obsessively, with my dad's industrial measuring tape, despairing at every centimetre I grew.

For the two years following my initial diagnosis of scoliosis, I underwent numerous physical examinations by male specialist doctors in West Perth and at the Shenton Park Rehabilitation Hospital. This scrutiny caused me further stress. The doctors lacked sensitivity – the first one I ever saw examined me alone for two hours and touched my breasts. He also had me photographed naked at the Royal Perth Hospital, which was a traumatic experience for me.

It was never suggested to my parents by any of these medical professionals that I receive therapy of any kind to assist in my physical and emotional wellbeing. It was simply reiterated that my condition was irreversible and there was nothing they could do to help me.

Traumatised by these examinations and the teasing at school, I developed a strong perception that my adolescence had spawned a monster. I felt swept up in a tsunami of anxiety concerning others' opinions of me. It was not, however, until I was sixteen that I saw my contorted figure in profile and from the back. Before then, I simply hadn't realised the extent of my condition, as it hadn't been explained to me adequately enough.

When I was in the bath I had felt, with my hand, a bulge on my back and became frightened. When I looked at my deformity in the mirror I was shocked, having never noticed it before. A feeling of devastation struck at my heart.

I thought, *This must be the ugliness the doctor had been referring to* – recalling his words from a time before.

"You didn't want to be a model anyway, did you?" he'd said flippantly while observing me.

"No," I lied.

Now I agreed with him – shivering on the bathroom mat – too afraid to look at myself in the mirror again. *God got me wrong somehow. I am an abnormality.*

No wonder all those doctors and their entourage of students would come in and stare at me, with great fascination.

I had inherited a template for grief from my family and so I rapidly descended into the darkest feelings of loss and despair. I became completely consumed by self-pity.

When alone, the full brunt of my personal tragedy overwhelmed me. *What man will ever love me this way?* Many times I wanted to die and go 'home' to God but I loved my family too much to suicide. I thought, in particular, my father couldn't bear any more grief in his life.

To relieve the mounting tensions inside me I sobbed into my pillow and through my heartache, spoke to God. I begged, promised, negotiated, demanded and sometimes raged for things to be different. With everything I had within me, I prayed for a miracle. But every morning when I awoke to place my hand upon my back, the feeling of deformity remained there and I believed that God had overlooked me.

I wondered, often, *Am I being punished by God? Am I not worthy of happiness? What is God's purpose for me? What is God – exactly?*

I sincerely desired to know myself and God better. Then, quite unexpectedly – God responded. I mustn't have thought it very likely – *Didn't God have better things to do than to visit me, personally?* Well, apparently not… and for this I am ever so grateful.

Of the six subjects I had in upper-high school, I enjoyed doing art the most. I poured over my projects for hours and time passed quickly. This suited my meticulous and fastidious nature. It was also an outlet for the intensity of emotion that dwelt within me. I felt the same kind of satisfaction from drawing, painting and mixing colours, as an athlete does running long and hard outdoors, except my pleasure was derived from my imagination running freely. Otherwise life as a teenager had its limitations.

Late one Sunday afternoon I was entranced in a drawing assignment when I heard my mum calling me. I pretended not to notice. I was too absorbed in my art to respond.

"Linda," mum called again. I ignored her. "… Linda."

With annoyance I muttered to myself, that if what she had to tell me was of importance then she could come out to see me. I had no intention of stopping my creative flow. Furthermore, I hoped it wasn't some boring chore she had in mind for me like folding the socks and undies. Sunday was laundry day. Mum spent the entire day washing, hanging and then ironing clothes – and complaining that we didn't do enough to help out.

"How will you know how to care for your husband and children one day," she'd say.

"I will *not* marry," I'd reply, wanting to get a rise out of her. I succeeded in this every time.

"Linda," she called yet again.

"What?" I yelled.

I was sitting with my legs tucked under me on the floor of mum's home office, hunched over papers and art supplies. The office was a demountable in the backyard, separate from the main house. I liked to do my art here as there was plenty of space to sprawl out.

"Linda," mum persisted, calling me from the house.

"What!" I yelled out, irritated.

"Linda."

I sighed and reluctantly stood up. My limbs felt heavy with numbness and I walked awkwardly over to the sliding door, opening it.

"What do you want?" I called through the flyscreen. There was no reply.

"What do you want?" I called, more loudly.

Mum finally appeared at the back door. "What do you want?" she asked through the flyscreen.

"Why are *you* calling *me*?" I said, shortly.

"I'm not calling you," she retorted.

"Oh… really?" I said, surprised. "Who is then?"

"There is no one calling you," she said. "It is only you and me at home, no one else. I cannot hear anyone calling you." Then she retreated into the house.

I must have imagined it. But was almost positive someone was calling me. Now I couldn't hear it anymore so I returned to my art work. A few minutes passed, then once more I could clearly hear someone calling my name. *Who is that?* I strained to listen.

"Linda."

I simply couldn't tell who it was. It was mystifying. Again they called. I went over to the sliding door, opened it and stepped outside into the sunlight. I felt its warmth on my face. It was a beautiful sunny day – the blue sky sprawled leisurely above. Birds fluttered and chirped about the garden.

I looked about and could see clearly that there was no one around, just me. I was now more curious than before to know exactly who it was calling me and why. If it wasn't my family, then perhaps it was a neighbour. It would be totally out of the ordinary, though, as they did not call anymore.

I walked to the side of our house and peered down the long pathway leading to the gate that was closed, as I expected it would be. I saw through the gate rails, there was no activity out the front either. *How very strange* – but I knew I wasn't imagining it.

Perhaps Craig is calling me? We hadn't spoken for years but maybe there was something he really needed to talk to me about regarding homework – as we were in the same year at school. We had once been the closest friends on earth but puberty severed our ties.

I peered over the fence. Craig was not there. I recalled how when I was five I told his mum over this fence that I would marry Craig one day. I lingered a little to look about his backyard. I hadn't looked for some time. I felt nostalgic pulls at my heart as I recalled the fun we shared playing there. I missed those wonderful carefree days. I missed Craig.

I stepped back into my backyard. Whoever it was, wasn't calling me anymore. *Oh well, it's back to my homework.* Sitting on my legs on the floor, hunched over my drawing, it started up again. *Blimey! Who is that calling me?* I couldn't even tell what direction they were calling from. I couldn't tell if it was a male or female?

"Linda," it spoke.

Certainly it was a casual, friendly way of saying my name. "Linda," it spoke again.

Then I recognised that the voice I heard was in the room with me. I held my breath. But I was the only one in the room?

"Linda," said the voice, close by me.

Well, apparently not! … I almost fainted with fright.

"Linda," it said, right next to me.

My heart skipped a beat.

"Linda," it said, closer than my breath.

I felt a wave of heat pass through my body; my hairs stood on end. I have never in all my life moved as quickly as I then did. I gathered all my belongings in one swoop and sprinted out of that room. *OH MY GOD!!! What was that?* I threw open the back door to the house and hurried inside.

"Mum," I called, "Mum, where are you!" The back door slammed behind me.

I heard mum in the kitchen, cooking dinner. I hurried to be close to her. I put all my things down on the dining table and sat down with a thud, my held-in breath escaping finally.

"What's for dinner?" I said, trying to act casually.

"Roast," she said, occupied by her task at the kitchen bench.

"Sounds yum," I said, my heart pounding violently in my chest.

"Don't put your things there," mum complained, looking up. "Your dad will be home soon. Help me set the table."

"Ok," I said. *Anything but return to the office, ever again.*

I never told mum about the 'calling of my name' incident, she wouldn't have believed me. If by chance she had believed me, she would have been afraid. I didn't know how to explain it. Yes, it was extraordinary but what did it mean? Why was something 'invisible' calling me? It was spooky. And I might have forgotten about it in time, putting it down to a vivid imagination, if it wasn't for yet another amazing event a few short months later.

While in church, I was usually on my knees with my eyes closed in prayer, when I pictured God in my mind. I imagined a beautiful white, fluffy cloud in a clear blue sky, radiating rainbow colours, with Jesus – neatly robed in pristine white cotton, his blonde hair resting gently upon his shoulders, his twinkling blue eyes and glowing pale skin – hovering in the middle of it. I was on the ground somewhere, looking up at this radiant scene.

During all the dull sermons our congregation endured, I never once heard a priest say that we laypeople had the power to be airborne like Jesus, or to exist in two places at once. But this is exactly what happened to me. I was sixteen when I had my first out-of-body experience. I didn't know to call it this, but it was the first of many airborne adventures I would have in time. It was the start of my spiritual awakening and the healing of the grief that pervaded my mind.

One night, I studied late and went to bed after midnight. I was in the early stages of sleep when I suddenly awoke to an electrifying vibration resonating throughout my entire body. Even though this sensation was warm and pleasant, like a gentle hum, I was alarmed by it, as it was like nothing I had experienced before.

I went to get up from bed but realised I couldn't move any part of my body, not even a little – I was completely paralysed. With all the might I could muster, I tried to move my legs but couldn't. I tried to move my arms but couldn't; … my tongue, to call out for help, but couldn't. I felt completely trapped.

Then amidst the mounting fear, I became aware of myself fluid and alert elsewhere in the room. I knew certainly that I was also not of my body. This was unbelievable to me, and my mind struggled to comprehend how this could be. How could I exist in two places at the same time – of my body and not of my body? I felt more frantic than before, like a fish out of water – my thoughts flapping about furiously. Somehow, I was split in two.

My heart sounded like a drum in my ears. Yet, another part of me was calm and lucid – unperturbed by the commotion stirring. This me, who was at peace, hovered beneath my bedroom ceiling to the right of the room, very near to the doorway. There, I felt lighter than the air. There too, I observed light seeping out from the slightly ajar bathroom door and dappling the carpeted floor with colour. So it was that I was seeing with a second set of eyes.

From the bathroom came the sounds of my mum washing her face and brushing her teeth. Then, quickly the experience passed.

I felt the airborne me swoop down like a bird and rejoin my body. As it did, the warm vibrations ceased and I began to move my fingers. Then the rest of my body came back to life, much to its own relief.

"Mum," I called out in the darkness for reassurance. It was enough to hear myself speak.

My limbs felt so heavy compared to the sheer weightlessness of what I recognised to be my spirit. I lay in bed utterly amazed by what had just transpired as fear and wonder rolled over me in waves.

Mum opened the bathroom door and flicked off the light. "Goodnight," she said to me in the darkness, as she walked by my room.

"Goodnight," I said to her. I turned onto my side and went to sleep, but not before whispering a few hurried Our Fathers beneath the sheet.

THREE
CHALLENGES

AT UNIVERSITY, I studied politics with the intention of entering law, and I loved the life of a student, however at eighteen, I was riddled with anxiety.

Following multiple episodes of panic which would overcome me as I'd walk the corridors, during the first six months of my studies, I thought it was time enough I got a grasp on my fluctuating emotions. I didn't want to spend any more time hiding out in the library's toilet cubicles, trying to calm myself.

I realised, it didn't matter how many of mum's Zig Ziglar or Norman Vincent Peale tapes I listened to, self-depreciating thoughts ruled the roost in my mind and I needed help. Fortunately, Murdoch University was a progressive campus and provided a free counselling service for its students. I booked an appointment for myself.

It was a relief to be able to voice my troubles to someone outside of the family, in an attempt to make sense of my thoughts, but the process of self-analysis didn't quash my feelings of anxiety – these persisted. It did allow me the opportunity to speak about the two supernatural events that had occurred to me aged sixteen, which had made a notable impression upon me. Thankfully, the psychologist was openminded enough to accept the validity of my experiences and did not consider these to be symptoms of a mental illness.

After a few counselling sessions, she thought I would benefit by talking to a psychic healer whom the psychologist had been to see.

"Clare's a remarkable intuitive," she assured me, "and she will be able to help you in ways that I cannot."

I had never heard of a psychic healer before this and I was a little apprehensive to meet with Clare. However, because it was the university psychologist who had recommended her to me, I decided to make an appointment and I visited Clare at her home.

The view from Clare's lounge room was breathtaking – it was of the Swan River and the metropolis in the distance. Tall water reeds and water birds with long thin legs moved with the breeze in the foreground, like music notes against a perfect blue sky. And upon the horizon the city buildings shimmered like an encrusted bracelet.

I turned my back on the inspiring scene and followed Clare down a short hallway to a small room with two comfortable armchairs. A stream of sunlight cascaded through a small open window where an incense stick smoked alongside oriental ornaments on a short-legged black table. We sat quietly for a moment and then Clare began to speak.

"Who very close to you talks about dying a lot?" she asked, placing a hand on her heart, "… says they're going to die?"

Her sudden gesture almost toppled me from my seat. I momentarily paused to process her accurate words. It was rather extraordinary to me that she should know *that*. How could she – I'd never mentioned *that* to the psychologist.

"M… my dad," I stammered, clenching my jaw, my heart

pounded in my chest. "When I was little... he believed he was dying. He'd say: 'I'm going to Karrakatta (cemetery)' – from his armchair, a hand to his heart – just like you're doing."

Her hand to her heart evoked strong memories of my dad who would sometimes sit in his armchair and sigh, with his hand to his heart – seeing this always upset me.

"Is he dying?" Clare asked me, her grey bob, neat and still.

"No – but he almost did," I explained. "He still sometimes thinks he is about to... die."

"He sighs a lot," she said.

I agreed – nodding my head. "But he can be cheery too," I interjected, "he likes to joke. He goes in and out of it."

"You sigh a lot too," she remarked.

"Do I?" I said, feeling self-conscious.

"Are you mourning someone?" she asked me.

"I don't think so," I said – though, in retrospect, I was mourning quite a lot about my life.

"You've taken on your dad's suffering," she said, conclusively. And this was something I'd never considered before.

"Does he have sudden outbursts?" she asked, perceptively.

"Well, he was traumatised by war," I explained.

"Do the outbursts upset you?" she pursued me.

"Well, yes," I acknowledged.

"I sense other issues there too, with your body, but it's your dad's suffering that has deeply affected you and this is the underlying cause of your anxiety."

"Ok... " I said, rather stunned – the woman just seemed to see straight into the heart of the matter.

She knew me better than I knew myself.

"You feel a lot of anxiety?" she asked, knowingly.

"Yes I do... how do you know these things?" I queried.

"I hear a voice," she explained. "It tells me what's really going on with people, so I can help them."

"Really?" – I was fascinated. "Um… I've heard a voice too," I told her, cautiously.

"Yes," she said.

"It was calling my name."

"That was Spirit," she said, assuredly.

But why? I thought.

"Think of it as your wake-up call," she explained. "It's nothing to be afraid of."

"Have you experienced it too?"

"I have. It was during the birth of my daughter – when I almost died."

Despite the counselling I received and the insight I'd gained by it, I continued to feel challenged. I focused diligently on my studies at which I excelled, receiving a scholarship to study politics at the University of North Carolina, at Chapel Hill in the United States, the following year – and then an internship to study human rights at the Australian National University, and in the Australian Federal Parliament, the year following that. I was very ambitious and well on my way to achieving the kind of success I thought would make me happy.

My parents financed my lifestyle. I had fulfilled their hope for me, of a higher education. This, they also believed, would ensure my future happiness. However appreciative I felt of their love and generosity, our relationship was strained and we argued quite regularly, particularly mum and I – we had done so since I was eight, which is when she became very career orientated.

Mum was determined to better herself and to provide a better way of life for her daughters than she had experienced growing up in Croatia. Born following the Second World War, in Dalmatia, in a small village not far from my dad's small village, she emulated the courage, resolve and sense of responsibility that was characteristic of her parents, from an early age.

Her father, Luka, was a resistance fighter during the war. Along with his two brothers, he spent years living in a network of caves throughout the mountainous terrain, as a measure of clan preservation. The men survived their ordeal, but their parents were shot dead at home.

During the war her mother, Mila, was a messenger. A message was scribed on a little piece of paper and rolled up like a cigarette, then platted into her hair, where it was concealed, and delivered to resistance fighters in the thick of night.

One day Mila and her mother Pera were in the field when they encountered a militia man who accused Mila of being a messenger – which she denied. Pera begged the man to spare her only child's life (who'd she'd conceived following seven miscarriages), telling him, she was merely a village girl going about her daily labours. Convincing him, Mila's life was spared – thus the young woman didn't suffer the same fate as her father, who'd been executed along with other villagers.

Following the war, Mila gave birth to her first child, a daughter, who died at two weeks from spinal complications. My mum was born next and her name was derived from a greeting, meaning good health and happiness. Good health she enjoyed, but happiness was hard to come by. She was reared on lack and trauma and had listened anxiously to stories retold about family members being executed, dying from agonising wounds and infection; of beatings and rapes; of villagers burnt alive in their houses, unable to escape – the screaming – the pleading; of scarcity and of mind-numbing fear.

Fearful of a similar fate, mum left her village, as a teenager, for the city of Zagreb where she took up work as a housekeeper for a prominent politician and attended secretarial college. It was also her task to transcribe the politician's manuscripts, as he was an avid and highly regarded political writer; the author of books. However, he often forgot to feed her and she resorted to eating the meagre scraps from his plate.

One winter, he and his film-star wife went abroad and mum gave all the wood belonging to them to her neighbour. The lady, named Pepica, didn't have any wood to burn and feared for her baby's life. The thick snow was mounting high against the outer walls of the ground floor apartment in which they lived, making it damp within.

After class each day, mum spent her time sitting with her neighbour and sharing the warmth. Pepica, who was ever grateful to mum for sharing her wood, always saved mum a bowl of soup and a little meat – a rare delicacy. In this way, their friendship blossomed.

Pepica was a teacher who worked with speech-impaired children but, as mum was to discover, she was also a very gifted psychic. She gave mum a very accurate reading of her future, out of the muddied granules of a coffee-cup.

"In three years, you will meet your husband," Pepica assured her. "You will be eighteen – then you will go live overseas together and leave this all behind you. It will be a much better life."

From these unlikely beginnings, the little mountain girl who herded goats and sheep, my mother, became one of Australia's most successful encyclopaedia sellers, receiving many accolades throughout the 1980s and 1990s.

This brought our family many benefits, but I missed my mum's company and attention. She worked a great deal, driven by powerful memories of lack, ever determined to improve our lot in life – and when she was at home, her thoughts were often occupied with her work or tasks at hand.

Both my parents, both very hardworking and dealing with a number of challenges, were stretched and tired. Arguing was how it played out between them – and this bickering caused me considerable displeasure.

As a young adult, I harboured resentments towards them, for being complicated emotionally and too busy to have noticed my condition of scoliosis developing. Had they, I reasoned, perhaps it might have been prevented in some way.

I was mistaken in this belief. However this sentiment persisted in me, that is, until I came 'face-to-face' with The Light at twenty-one. From that extraordinary moment forward – the way in which I perceived the circumstances of my life – my history, identity, body, relationships and purpose, changed dramatically.

FOUR
ULTIMATE POWER REALITY

SOMEONE IS SITTING *on my bed. I must be dreaming.* My bed sheet gently pulled away from me. Very quickly I became wide awake, with all my senses on high alert. *Did I imagine it?* I wasn't quite sure, so I waited for the smallest, telling sign, hoping that I had.

As I lay very, *very* still, I pretended to be asleep and I held my breath.

Then my bed sheet pulled away from me a little more. My heart thumped so violently with fright, it was all I could hear, but I didn't dare move. *What am I going to do?*

I lived alone, and there should not have been anyone sitting at the end of my bed in the middle of the night, not even a dog – I didn't have a pet. However, I could feel someone sitting there, for sure.

Who is that? I thought, panicked, still too afraid to breathe or to look. My mind convulsed. *Will my neighbours hear me if I scream for help? What if they don't hear me? What if I open my mouth and not a sound comes out, because it is stifled by fear, like in a terrible nightmare?*

My thoughts raced around in circles frantically trying to find a way out of this unfortunate situation, but I knew my options were gravely limited. Then I felt another gentle pull of the sheet. This time, I couldn't pretend it didn't happen because it *really* did. Someone wanted me to wake up and for me to know that they were present.

There was only one way out of the bedroom and it was past whoever was sitting on my bed. I simply had to confront my intruder, so I finally took courage, sat bolt upright and looked straight ahead – but there was no one to see. It was baffling.

There was no one to see yet still I could feel someone sitting at the end of my bed! They were weighing down the mattress. *What the…?* Before I could give it another thought, a most extraordinary light took hold of my attention. It hovered above the foot of my bed, in mid-air. I didn't see it appear, it was just suddenly there.

I then became aware of two spiritual presences in my bedroom: the invisible one sitting on my bed and the spectacular, airborne luminosity. Of the two, the luminosity completely entranced me.

It was the most astonishing configuration I'd ever seen. It was breathtaking! I knew with absolute certainty that the light was 'God' – before a thought could even form in my mind, though God appeared differently to what I imagined God might look like. Some part of me was so familiar with 'The Light' that it simply rejoiced in the reunion.

The Light I observed was approximately one and a half metres wide. At its centre was a black circular void and from this, reaching outward, were spectacular arcs of light, as a whole, forming a perfect circle.

The circle of light rotated clockwise and pulsated with extraordinary power, yet stood still in mid-air. It was brighter than the sun, yet I could look upon it. Had I been seeing it with my bare human eyes, these would surely have been burnt out. Thus, I have since reasoned, I must have been seeing it with spiritual eyes.

The Light was alive and aware. It was without form, gender,

age, race or creed. It was perfect unconditional love and it longed to be united with me as much as I longed to be united with it. It possessed an extraordinary, unforgettable magnetism that entered me through my heart.

As I was sitting up in bed and facing The Light, I felt a great force pulling on me, in rhythm with the pulsations emanating from it. A great throb swelled in my heart, permeating my entire self, again and again. I could barely breathe with the unearthly pleasure. The throbs lapped at me like waves on a shore, rising up my neck and into my head, causing tears to pour out of my eyes, uncontrollably.

It was the ultimate celestial orgasm and I felt like a cup overflowing with plenty. The pulse of God moving through me brought such intense pleasure that I felt I might burst like the ripest berry in the sun. I almost couldn't stand to feel such rapture and then it was as if my mind exploded. I burst out of the confines of my thoughts and into the highest stratosphere of consciousness.

Everything here was bright white light. There was nothing other than The Light of God. I had entered the ultimate heaven. I even became the ultimate heaven. I was spiritual completion. I was perfect love. God and I were one. There were no reflections – no point of reference. There was no thought. Thought could not and did not exist in this no-space.

God simply was. God simply is. 'I' was not. God was 'I Am' without the 'I'. God was 'Am'.

There was no here, no there, no Linda, no other. Light and silence existed in no place and in no time, and everything that ever was, is, will and could be, was of The Light and The Silence.

The Silence was perfect tranquillity yet it hummed with extreme power. In the complete stillness God was perpetually in motion. God was stillness and motion at the same time, in no-time.

This was the ultimate power reality. There was no higher-power

– no vaster reality – any greater wisdom – and no greater potential. Nothing greater existed anywhere and nowhere. It was the end point and the beginning point. I could have stayed like this forever, never wanting for anything. I was completely fulfilled and at peace.

I don't know how long I was in this boundless paradise. It felt like an eternity. Then my awareness returned to my bedroom and still it was night.

I was in bed yet again, not alone. I suddenly became aware of a third spiritual presence. I had recently desired a lover but not of the ethereal kind. My companion was a ghost, lying naked at my right side. Ordinarily, I would have bolted at such an eerie sight but, on this occasion, instead I felt compelled to observe him. I didn't feel in any kind of danger. The spirit seemed quite unaware of me.

Remarkably, I could see the wardrobe doors through him. He was transparent grey, tall, had a beard and a head of wavy hair. He was perhaps forty earthly years in appearance but because he looked so sickly, it was hard to tell exactly – he may have been younger. He was so emaciated that I could see his ribs protruding and his arms were long and thin. I felt great pity for him.

He was not anyone I recognised. It was evident that in earthly life he had suffered much and he was suffering still. Emotionally, and in thought, he had not let go of his suffering though the physical life had released him, and he had not yet transitioned into The Light. It was apparent that he existed in his own hell.

Mostly, it was his eyes that took my attention. These were bright red and exemplified his grief. His eyes stared lifelessly at the ceiling. I didn't know what he saw there, if anything, of the room. I felt deep depression emanating from this disembodied man. I didn't feel he was evil but, rather, that he was lost. He was suffering a great separation from God in his own mind, though God was right before him and had always been there. He was not seeing, not acknowledging The Light of his own being.

I felt God loving him unconditionally. The power would wait for him, however long it took, so he could complete his transition to a heavenly state – to a higher experience of existence.

I fell asleep again, as if I had seen all I was supposed to see. In the morning I awoke, recalling all that had transpired in the night, the memory of which has never faded for me.

I mulled endlessly over my encounter with The Light and my rational mind dissected every segment of this grand and unexpected event in my life. Questions sprouted up in me like wildflowers. The most persistent one being, why did God visit *me*?

The day following my life-changing encounter, I felt I had to speak to someone about it, so I drove to a Buddhist monastery near my home. The Catholics I knew didn't speak about this kind of thing. I was apprehensive that a priest would construe the ghost with red eyes as evil, when I felt this wasn't so.

I arrived at the Buddhist monastery in Mount Lawley to learn that the three monks usually residing there were travelling overseas and wouldn't be back for three weeks. I returned to my car, disappointed yet determined to speak with someone so I drove next into the city, to the main Catholic Cathedral – Saint Mary's.

I would attempt to speak to a priest about what had happened to me the previous night and hoped I would be believed. I walked into the administration office and asked the secretary if I could speak with a priest.

"Yes, Father will soon be available," she said kindly. "Come with me."

She led me to a small, tidy room where I waited for counsel. After only a few moments the priest appeared.

"Hello Father," I said a little anxiously, as he took his seat across from me.

"What would you like to discuss with me today?" he asked.

"Father," I spoke up, "last night, I was woken from my sleep to God's presence in my room. God appeared to me as a spectacular white light. I want to understand why God visited me?"

"Describe this light to me," he said, unmoved, and I described the specific configuration and qualities of The Light to Father. Then I went on to describe my experience of the ultimate heaven, and of returning from bliss to a ghost, and my thoughts about it. Father listened carefully and then he responded.

"The Catholic Church is only interested in hearing about visions of Christ or the Blessed Mother or incidences of stigmata," he stated plainly. Then he paused. His pause was like a big full stop imprinted on my forehead and I began to sweat. *Where to from here?* I thought.

Father stood up and extended his arm over my head while I remained seated. He placed his hand, palm down upon my hair and recited a prayer, that I am certain was for the purpose of dispelling any evil spirit that may have lodged between my ears. It wouldn't have then surprised me, if he'd dug both his hands deep into his pockets and retrieved a few knobs of garlic to hang around my neck.

"Thank you Father," I said politely, however, I left feeling very disappointed. Aside from the humiliation of it, which was rather short lived, I felt sad that an elder of my faith had denied the reality of the most powerful spiritual experience of my life. For this reason, and others, I felt it was time for this sheep to diverge from the flock. I had finally grown the courage and determination to experience 'the ultimate power' in the universe, in my own way.

In time, I saw this incident with the priest as a blessing because it propelled me forward into my own personal spirituality, and brought about a greater intimacy between myself and the source of life. God was no longer a notion in a book or a string of words belonging to some man dressed in a ceremonial robe – the experience of God now belonged to me.

I slept with the lamp on at night for six months after my encounter with the red-eyed ghost. Even though when I experienced him I was without any fear, afterwards my mind struggled with the idea that he could still be in my bed at night, sleeping next to me. I wondered often, why I had encountered this gloomy spirit. Why had God opened my spiritual eyes to this lost soul? Was I supposed to help him in some way? I prayed for his healing, thinking this might help him to move on. I prayed for his spiritual awakening. I prayed for his transition into heaven.

The red-eyed ghost taught me a vital life-lesson – that whatever a person feels and thinks, they carry it over with them into the afterlife. There is no avoiding one's self, in life or in death. And that God is a perpetual companion of every soul.

✺

There had never before been an experience in my life that had caused me such personal fulfilment as my encounter with The Light. I longed to be reunited with this power again – to feel so good – so loved – so accepted. And I was most fortunate, to have two more experiences of The Light in the months to follow, in which I travelled, in spirit, through a tunnel towards a great luminosity at an awesome speed. The Light possessed all the extraordinary qualities I'd experienced before.

Upon both these occasions I don't have a memory of what happened once I entered The Light, but since then I have painted many pictures of my out-of-body journeys which read like heavenly postcards.

From my Light experiences, I developed an insatiable appetite for spiritual knowledge. Although previously I'd been consumed with thoughts of getting ahead academically and professionally, and materially, this shifted. I became completely preoccupied with The Light – and with returning to it.

In the weeks and months that followed these inspiring events, I would sometimes break down in tearful sorrow, because the world felt harsher and noisier than ever before. The contrast between the dysfunctions of humanity and God's love was extreme, and I hardly knew how to deal with it; aside from spending more time at home, with the television and radio switched off. Sometimes, I still wished to be rid of this life, so I could return to my real home, in heaven, where I felt complete.

The few people I entrusted my spiritual experiences to, through no fault of their own, couldn't grasp the magnitude of what had happen to me.

It was not until the following year, at age twenty-two, that I had the intense direct-lived out-of-body experience of a life review and preview. From that time on I never again had the feeling of wanting to die – of wanting to escape the circumstances of my earthly life. This mind-blowing event anchored me to my physical life and completely transformed me – all the psychiatrists in the world couldn't have formulated a more effective and far-reaching remedy. I gained a remarkable sense of purpose that has never abated. I suddenly felt my life really mattered – to me and to others.

I came to accept my physicality, overnight. Not my disfigurement – not quite yet – but my humanness, my humanity. I felt it was perfectly ok to be 'flawed'. I understood that my condition of scoliosis, for all the upset it had caused me, was meaningful – a gift. Indeed my personal challenges had been a catalyst for meaningful change in my life. My encounters with The Light, and my life review and preview, caused me to acknowledge that reality is far more complex and wondrous than is allowed for by the human mind.

FIVE
LIFE REVIEW & PREVIEW

I T WAS NIGHT when I arrived at the house. The front door was wide open and I knew to go inside. I entered a dimly lit hallway and was immediately drawn to three framed pictures on the wall. I went up to the first one to take a closer look and was astonished to see – *the picture was of me.*

This was most unexpected, not that I had been expecting anything in particular. The quality of the picture was fascinating to see and further enhanced my amazement. It appeared to glow from within. The entire image was made of light. It was utterly magical.

It was not Linda I saw in the picture but a different woman entirely, yet I knew absolutely, she was me. The moment allowed for extraordinary perception, a heightened sense of knowing the truth – as if the picture itself was alive, intelligent and communicating with me. I was utterly transfixed by the woman of fair complexion and from a different lifetime to the one I am living now. She appeared very real to me; that is, she was three-dimensional. I might have reached into the picture and touched her and felt her pale living flesh, soft and warm, as I might have with any other living human being standing before me. It was as if I was peering at her across the way, through a small window in the wall, where she lived in a parallel time and space. We were both alive, simultaneously, so it seemed to me.

I was then drawn to the second framed picture along the wall and, again, saw myself. I was another woman from yet another lifetime. She too was very much alive. I marvelled at her as I did the first woman. I might have reached into this picture and touched her too, had I not been attracted to the third and final picture on the wall.

As I stood before the last picture, I was once more amazed to see a third woman I had been from yet another lifetime. She too was very much alive. I couldn't discern if these women were alive in spirit or of the flesh. They appeared physical, however they also appeared illuminated from within.

Like the others, the third woman too was off in the distance, though near enough for me to see the features of her clothing. She wore a long, full skirt covering her legs entirely and a modest blouse, her hair was pinned up on top of her head.

I shared a quiet, intimate moment with each of them, while they contemplated their heartfelt longings. I observed that they were plump women and it surprised me that I have been full figured, because in my current life, especially as a teenager, I had such concerns over being too thin.

Then, in an instant, I gained remarkable clarity of mind. I understood that each of these women had disliked their physical bodies and had longed to be tall and lean. This yearning in each of them, in three different lifetimes, created my current form. Their thoughts and feelings manifested their 'future' self. I was amazed that the tall, lean body I had come to loathe in this current lifetime had been desired by me entirely – and that my thoughts and feelings were so creative and powerful.

I've been plump, I thought, in amazement. Then I heard laughter bounding down the hallway. I looked to see who was making this unexpected sound and saw a full-figured woman approaching me.

"Yes, you have been (plump)," she smiled at me.

I was amazed this woman could read my thoughts. She was communicating with me but her lips where not moving. I could sense her joy at seeing me. The emotion was emanating from her as power and it permeated my entire being.

Suddenly I recognised her as my very dear friend. It was as if a shroud of forgetfulness had been lifted from me and it became a celebration between us. We embraced as the very best of friends, having not seen one another for the longest time. I sensed that I knew her from well before my current lifetime. I felt immense spiritual love for my friend and she for me. Our love vibrated between and within us as we quite literally merged into each other. The love was a warm spiritual substance made of light and I could see it and sense it. And it was only then that I realised we were made of this miraculous substance – we were made of light!

My friend led me from the hallway into an adjacent sitting room where we sat in armchairs, opposite one another. It was then I noticed she had an item in her hands – like a clipboard, that she was concentrating on.

"In your life," she began matter of factly, looking at me, "you have felt anger, fear, resentment, sadness…" and she went on to list all the negative moods I had ever experienced.

"How do you feel about your relationship with your parents?" she asked me.

In the pause that existed between her question and me considering it, my breadth of awareness expanded dramatically. I could perceive my life experiences in every conceivable way, like a teacup magically being able to hold the contents of the entire ocean.

I was able to perceive the truth with 360-degree vision, from the outside and the inside, from the top and the bottom, from the left and the right. I was able to see my life at many different levels, down to the tiniest particle. Not only what it was made of, but also how it feels. Sensing it in every way imaginable, and then in ways unimaginable to the human mind – knowing from where it had evolved and to where it was evolving and much, much more, all simultaneously and in an instant.

I observed everything that had ever transpired between me and my parents. That is, from my perspective, their perspectives, and every other person's perspective who had ever had a thought or feeling on the matter of my relationship with my parents.

Then I entered a state of divine self-assessment.

I can reveal there was no high-in-the-sky, paternal power-figure with thunderbolts in his hair, ready to judge my deeds on earth and to deliver his wrath upon me for my numerous shortcomings. Rather, I was to judge myself, but from an elevated perspective.

In this moment, I was utterly present to myself – to my highest wisdom, to my highest spiritual aspect. I couldn't have fooled myself, even if I'd tried to, about the truth of that which I was and had been. I held only the overwhelming desire to make a clear, honest assessment of every single one of my life experiences as my parents' youngest daughter.

I experienced a thorough review of my interactions with my parents and discovered that our relationship was absolutely perfect – as it is, and as it had been. Yes, we may have had our challenges from time to time but our relationship served a spiritual purpose. We were together in our relationship to learn, to grow, to love, and to expand in consciousness. I knew there was great meaning to every single one of our interactions. We had chosen to be a family before we made a transition from the spiritual realm to earthly life. We were in perfect spiritual harmony.

Furthermore, it was made apparent to me that everything in my earthly life that had transpired and was yet to transpire, down to the smallest and most inconsequential occurrence was incredibly powerful, valuable and ordered. I discovered there is absolutely nothing haphazard about life. The universe reverberates with methodical arrangement. It is a master symphony. I understood that all earthly experiences contributed to divine knowledge; all souls contribute to the expansion of other souls.

"Do you want to stay here with me?" my friend asked me.

Is it my choice? I thought, amazed.

"It can be arranged," she assured me.

I felt astonished that it was my choice to stay or not to stay in this magical place with my magical friend. *How can it be arranged? If I choose to stay, will my body just die in bed or will I forget I had this profound experience and, one day soon, unexpectedly die due to illness or an accident?*

I looked at my friend and a powerful longing arose in me, to remain with her and to be free of my earthly burdens – but I paused to consider my family. I felt a responsibility to them.

"I couldn't do it to my father," I told her. "He wouldn't be able to cope without me."

"He'd be fine," she assured me. "So would your mother and sister. Life would go on for them."

I was surprised by her certainty on this, but before I could give it another thought my awareness expanded to awesome proportions. An exceedingly spectacular light show appeared before me, taking up my entire view.

It was as if I had been granted a gold-ticket seat in the cinema of my potentiality. From this vantage point, I observed my future in every detail. The experiences I was yet to live were revealed to me as three-dimensional images, alive, though larger than life, and these flickered before me at a roaring pace. It required all of my focused attention to absorb all that I sensed.

It was an extraordinary multi-sensory, multi-faceted telecast. I experienced the spiritual purpose for which I was born. I discovered my life was planned entirely in the spiritual realm before it manifested on the physical plane. I learnt why only I could live my life and how valuable it was to other lives, and how intricately entwined my life was in the broad tapestry of universal life.

Experiencing my future caused an enormous sense of optimism and wellbeing to arise in me. I suddenly gained tremendous urgency and drive to get on with living my life authentically. When the life preview concluded, I longed to return to my human life so that I could fulfil my greater spiritual purpose.

"It's four o'clock," my friend said, looking at her watch. "I must go. We have many souls arriving."

I considered this unusual remark and looked to her questioningly, only then to realise, that my friend wasn't with me anymore. She had simply disappeared.

I noticed a door to my right, so I got up and went to it and slid it open. I stepped outside into a courtyard and saw that it was still night. A small group of people sat in a circle and I went to join them. A man spoke and his audience was captivated. I sat down next to a young woman – I didn't recognise any of the people I was amongst. The young woman I sat next to laughed at something the man had said and her sudden outburst shocked me. I thought her laughter sounded like that of a hyena. I looked at her and her mouth opened even wider, just like a hyena's. I was so startled by this – *did my thought cause the effect?* But before I could give it another thought, I felt myself descending, down, down, down, towards my body in bed.

I felt my spirit, lighter than the air, reconnect with my form. It was an *enormous* burden to be of the flesh again. I tried to hold the thought, in mind, that my body was actually a blessing. Nonetheless, I felt heavy, awkward and uncomfortable again. *How am I going to move this body? It feels so incredibly heavy – immovable even.* I focused my thought on the act of moving. Soon I was able to move a finger, just a little. I focused on moving all my fingers and they moved. My body began to come to life.

I rolled onto my side, sat up and got out of bed. I flicked on my bedroom light and sat back down in bed again. I looked at the clock radio. It displayed 4:00 am exactly, in bold red, electronic numbers. I retrieved pen and paper from a drawer next to me and made note of this truly phenomenal event.

SIX
SYNCHRONICITY

PERHAPS, ONE OF the most difficult things about perceiving an extraordinary reality is that many other people don't. Also, there's an invisible wall that goes up, often enough, when the word God is uttered in a sentence (less so when the word Spirit is spoken of).

God is a contentious topic for so many reasons.

I therefore have always found it difficult to share my spiritual experiences openly with others. I have met with a mood of apathy, disbelief or fear – even anger.

Following my first Light experience, I felt a compulsion to speak out about the magnificence I had experienced. I wanted people to know – an infinite power really exists that loves them, absolutely. However, my anxiety about speaking about it grew because, each time I tried to do so, I sensed I wasn't being understood.

Some people did listen, but they couldn't relate to the intensity I was feeling or appreciate just how very real these spiritual encounters were.

When I heard myself speaking of The Light, of bliss, of eternity… it sounded tame and small compared with the grand reality I had experienced.

In time, I stopped trying to explain to others the wondrous things I perceived. This created friction within me, which eventually gave rise to excruciating migraines (from the age of twenty-five). It took me ten years to make a connection between the throbbing pain in my head and my muted voice. I visited numerous practitioners, each with their own diagnosis and cure, and spent thousands of dollars on remedies that never alleviated the affliction.

Following my life review/preview experience, what I longed for, was to be able to make meaningful connections with people who had seen what I had seen and felt what I had felt, and been illuminated as I had been. Then one day I met someone in the most unusual of circumstances, who offered me further insight into the vast reality I had glimpsed. It was the kind of connection I had been longing for.

One autumn morning I entered a popular Perth city bookstore and made my way to the spirituality/self-help aisle. This was a relatively new pastime of mine. I quickly became immersed in browsing when a voice interrupted, urging me on to another bookstore along the mall.

I knew of this bookstore and it was the least inspiring bookstore I had ever seen. I ignored the voice, at first. It came from somewhere, but nowhere in particular, and I continued to read the back of the book I had in my hands.

"Go now!" the voice insisted.

I'm not going anywhere. I'm very happy right where I am.

"Go!" the voice urged me. "There's someone you *need* to meet."

Oh dear, am I being delusional? Now I seem to be hearing a voice that no one else can hear.

"Hurry," the voice said, "or you will miss him."

I'm staying put, I said to myself, though now I felt conflicted.

What if the voice is right? What if there is someone I need to meet in that very ugly bookstore.

To an onlooker I appeared as any ordinary browsing customer would – quiet, absorbed – but inside myself I was wrangling with an unknown presence.

"You need to go now!" the voice said.

Who is that talking to me?

I finally slipped the book back into its slot on the shelf and walked out of the store. Rather, I felt I was catapulted out of the store by an invisible force. I felt in a great hurry. It was all very strange, indeed.

Out on the open Hay Street mall I mixed in with the bustling mid-morning pedestrian traffic. I soon came to pause before the entrance to a quaint little arcade with decorative floor tiles, wondering if I should really go in.

The first shop on the arcade with frontage on the mall sold diamonds. The next shop along was tucked away behind a stairwell. It happened to be the tiniest bookstore in the world. I knew of this secondhand bookstore because I walked past it often enough, to get to the best shoe store in town. At most, the tiniest and most featureless bookstore ever to exist could only hold four people in it, uncomfortably, which included the man who managed it.

I walked along the arcade and reluctantly entered the store. I turned about on the spot to view all the books crammed high into tight spaces. As I did so, I observed the bookstore keeper. He was wearing the same mustard-coloured cardigan he always wore and the same dour expression.

"Hello," I said to him, cheerily.

It took a few seconds for the old man to look up at me from the dusty corner of his store. He then proceeded to say nothing, carrying on as he had been without any display of pleasure. I watched his grey head, stoop over the book again, as his body sat motionless in an old swivel chair behind a tiny desk.

One hardly knows the circumstances of his life, I thought.

A middle-aged woman was browsing the shelves very near to me, but I understood she was not the one I had come to meet. I then wondered what I should do next. Had I made a mistake coming here? I glanced over at a pile of used magazines, stacked high on an old kitchen chair and supported by the wall. I wondered who actually bought a used woman's magazine.

Perhaps I should leave. Nothing of any real interest held my attention. I felt very tall in this tiny space and rather self-conscious. Then a young man entered the store and began to browse a shelf, between the woman and the open door.

"He's the one," the voice said clearly. "Speak to him."

I'm not speaking to him, first, I insisted.

"Speak to him," it said again.

It felt very crowded in the store and I didn't know what to do. The fair-haired man was a complete stranger to me and he didn't take any notice of me whatsoever.

"It'll be ok. Speak to him," it urged me.

I hesitated. *What if I make an absolute fool of myself?* I so disliked the feeling of complete and utter humiliation. But the urge to speak to this stranger became so overwhelming that I blurted out a crude sound that broke the silence.

"Umm..." I said, arousing his attention, "They're telling me... that you have something important to share with me."

Hearing my own voice in such a setting almost shocked me to death. My heart raced wildly. I took a deep breath in and pointed at my head, like perhaps 'they' were dangling from my ears. *Who were 'they' anyway?* He looked at me intently and my stomach churned.

"Yes, I feel it too," he stated matter of factly, as if he too had been waiting for me. "Let us go somewhere else where we can talk more privately."

"Ok," I staggered, amazed, as I watched him return a book to the shelf. He picked up his rucksack, threw it over his right shoulder and we left the store together, walking side by side.

"There's a café I frequent on the other mall," he explained, as we walked out of the quaint arcade. "It's not far from here."

"Ok," I said. I didn't know what else to say. I felt awkward, relieved and intrigued all at once. We didn't speak for five minutes, not until we arrived at the café and sat down at a small table, outside in the sunshine. It was the longest pause of my life.

Sitting across from him, I noticed his eyes for the first time since we'd met. They were the bluest eyes I'd ever seen and they looked like crystals. They seemed to glow from within. His hair was cut close to his head, and his body was small and lean.

"My name is Paul," he said to me. "I'm an alchemist."

What? What's an alchemist?

"I'm Linda," I finally spoke.

"I was looking for a book on alchemy," Paul explained. "You never know what you might find in a place like that."

That's true, I agreed – nodding my head.

Our coffees arrived at the table and then I waited for the waiter to go before speaking again.

"I heard a voice telling me to meet you in that tiny bookstore," I explained myself, "… but I almost didn't go. I thought I might be imagining it."

"It's your inner counsel," he said, then leaning in a little closer. "My teacher said this would happen – that I would meet someone like you."

"*Really?*" I said, amazed, sipping my coffee with utter intrigue. It was definitely one of the more bizarre moments of my life.

"Meeting you like this is new to me," I revealed.

"Like energies attract," he said, drinking his coffee. "Do you know about synchronicity?"

"Not really," I said. "I mean… I've heard the word."

"Are you aware of seemingly unrelated events in your life aligning in such a way that is, *meaningful*?"

"Yes, increasingly so," I agreed.

"You meet a stranger, in a bookstore, yet the event turns out to be powerful – even life-changing?"

"Yes," I nodded my head.

"That's synchronicity. Did you come to town intending to meet an alchemist?"

"No – never," I said.

"I didn't come here intending to meet you either. But we did meet and it is meaningful – that's synchronicity," Paul continued, "you see, you attract things to yourself all the time, not just things but situations and people… your energy field does."

He must have read me like an open book because I didn't know what he meant by an energy field.

"You are an energy field – that is what you are – and you exist within a vast energy grid, in which you are connected to all other energy fields," he explained. "This interconnectedness between the energy fields makes subtle communications, like the inner-voice you heard, and synchronicities possible."

This guy is off the planet, I thought as I sipped my coffee. I glimpsed at the people walking by, along the mall, oblivious to our conversation.

"What exactly is an alchemist?" I asked Paul.

"An alchemist is someone who is capable of changing lead into gold," he told me. "However the real power of the alchemist is to be able to transform from flesh into spiritual substance – into high frequency energy. Then he or she is able to enter into higher dimensions of reality – to experience the ultra-reality. Some people call this state heaven but there's lots of different ways of describing it. This is what I'm learning to do with the guidance of my teacher – my *master* teacher."

"Is your teacher able to transform herself?"

"Yes, she is a master alchemist," he said.

"How does she do this?" I asked – most intrigued.

"Through meditation and other practices," he explained. "Have you found your master teacher yet?"

"I don't know what a master teacher is, really," I told him.

"It's the most significant spiritual teacher of your life," he explained. "Some people have more than one. Master teachers are very powerful beings and they're here, on the earth-plane, to help elevate our consciousness. You would have been their student in other life times too, as you'll be in future life times."

"Well, I'm not sure if I have," I said, thinking on it.

"You know it when you do… I did," Paul affirmed, pausing to take another sip of his coffee.

"Then I haven't… not yet," I said, wondering, if in fact, I ever would.

"Your master teacher is coming," he assured me, answering my thoughts.

How can he be so sure?

"I feel it," his eyes smiled.

"How will I know who this master person is?" I queried, doubting him.

"You'll feel it," Paul assured me. "You really will."

We left the café some two hours after we'd met in the tiny bookstore, having talked a good deal about spiritual matters. I also had the opportunity to share my spiritual experiences with Paul – of which he was very accepting.

We then walked together to a third bookstore – Paul's favourite one.

I had never been to this bookstore before, nor did I know of it prior to Paul taking me there. We went inside and I was amazed by its size – there were so many books. Paul guided me along its many shelves. These were completely devoted to spiritual, alternate reality and paranormal themes.

I realised then that there were many people on a quest for the truth of their existence – *I was not alone.*

In Paul's company I took a book from a shelf and looked over it for the shortest time. When I looked up from it, he was gone. We were too far from the store's entrance, for him to have made an exit in that time. I walked about the aisles looking for him but I never saw him again. I have since thought that perhaps he was not entirely of this world, but a messenger, heralding great things to come.

SEVEN
PSYCHIC DEVELOPMENT

SOON AFTER MY meeting with Paul the alchemist, I joined a psychic development group in Fremantle that was led by a trance medium named Claire. I was graduating from university, and I had no idea what a trance medium did – but I wanted to develop my burgeoning intuition.

Claire the trance medium was a happy, lively personality in her mid-thirties. She had bright red hair that she wore in pigtails, and a booming voice elevated her beyond her tiny stature. She wore bright free-flowing clothes, and tribal adornments decorated her arms and hair.

There were some fifteen people in the class, of varying ages and we sat together in a circle to meditate. Sitting cross-legged in quietude was new to me and I realised rather quickly that my mind just never kept still. I thought, *I'm thoroughly annoying myself. This is not relaxing at all.*

Following meditation and a short introduction from everyone – Claire entered a trance state. She explained to us prior to this that she would allow 'energies' access to her vocal cords by vacating her body willingly.

"Where do you go?" a man asked.

"I watch everything going on from there," she pointed to the corner of the room.

"Are you afraid a bad entity might enter your body?" a woman asked.

"No – I'm protected by my spirit guides," she said, assuredly.

I watched as Claire closed her eyes in the meditative posture. She breathed deeply and slowly. Her eyelids and face twitched a little, then she began to make some very strange sounds. I flicked an 'eyes-wide-as-saucers' glance around the group but no one took any notice of me. They all appeared to be taking Claire *very* seriously, so I too went along with it, though, really, all I wanted to do was to cackle with laughter!

"Jesus, Mary and Joseph!" I thought I heard my aunt exclaiming all the way from her kitchen sink, on the other side of town. My overriding thought was – *What a bloody racket.* Then – *this can't be for real. These people are completely bonkers!* Followed by – *I hope she can't read my thoughts.*

The strange sounds subsided and Claire began to speak in a slightly altered voice. However, it was not really Claire, but a friendly entity from a far-off planet, here to share wisdom with us… apparently. *Should I do a runner now?* I eyed off the emergency exit door, planning my potential route of escape. Instead – I sat still, cross-legged, fighting the urge to laugh, as all kinds of formless beings talked to us with Claire's vocal cords. They ranged from Native Americans to extra-terrestrials from star systems I'd never heard of.

At the end of the session I was in something of a quandary. I felt I didn't fit in here *at all* but I'd paid for the term in advance (I now realised why this had been a requirement) – so what was I to do?

I returned the following Saturday morning for another session of Claire's psychic development class, intrigued by all the strangeness. If nothing else, I coerced myself into believing; I'll learn how to meditate (even if the folks are a bit *crackers*).

We meditated, spoke about personal issues, performed psychic surgery that entailed cutting imaginary emotional ties with imaginary scissors, and listened to Claire share universal wisdom while in trance. I again wondered if she was having us on and if she was really just a bit – *crazy*.

During week three Claire spoke of every person having a spirit guide or a number of spirit guides who assisted us through life. I wondered if perhaps it had been my spirit guide speaking to me in the bookstore that day, urging me to meet Paul – or if spirit guides were baloney.

"Do you see Karen's spirit guide?" Claire asked the group. "He's showing himself to us beautifully."

"He's a Native American," a woman said.

That's original. Why a Native American? Why not a farmer from Norway?

"Yes," someone replied, "I see him."

"Yes," another person spoke up, "I see him too."

I looked at Karen expecting to see nothing out of the ordinary, when instead I observed the most intense golden light I've ever seen – which surrounded her entirely. Within this extraordinary other-world light sat none other than (yes) a Native American man – minus the feather-headdress.

I could hardly believe my eyes. *Bloody hell, this stuff is actually for real!* I watched for a couple of minutes, absolutely riveted, as the scene flickered between alternating visions of Karen and then the Native American – it was mind-blowing!

Then it finally happened one Saturday morning, as the weeks progressed, that I encountered The Light once again. I was lying on the floor having psychic surgery performed on me, with my eyes closed, when a beautiful white light grew in radiance until I was utterly transfixed by it. I felt love-struck. I described to Claire and the group what I was experiencing.

"That's Spirit," Claire spoke.

The Light filled me with an enormous sense of wellbeing. I didn't enter the ultimate power reality state, that I previously had, rather retaining my sense of individuality, but I knew, with certainty, that God/Spirit was alive *in me*.

Claire spoke again and this disrupted my focus – The Light then disappeared from my sight and I felt terribly disappointed that my experience of it was short-lived.

Following this I then experienced myself as a stillborn. I felt a cord wrapped about my neck and I found it impossible to breathe. I gasped for air.

"You're experiencing a past life," Claire stated, matter of factly, "take a deep, slow breath." The clairvoyants in the group reiterated what I was experiencing by sharing their visions of me as a stillborn. It was a strange experience. I took a deep breath and resumed this vital bodily function.

That afternoon, I visited my best friend Gil at his home in South Fremantle, who I had met during my last semester of university. I described my 'stillborn' experience to him.

"My mum delivered a stillborn child before I was born," Gil told me. "Perhaps you were *that* baby."

I didn't know. We did however share some uncanny coincidences – Gil, his mum and me. His mum and I had an undeniable connection.

Following the psychic development course, I saw Claire for a private consultation. She sat on a pillow in her usual meditative posture and closed her eyes. I sat in a chair opposite her, awaiting the spectacle to begin, not really knowing what to expect. Claire began making strange sounds and her eyes twitched. She took deep, slow breaths and then her head moved from side to side, as if she was looking around the room through her closed eyelids.

"Hello my beloved," she spoke softly and slowly – in trance.

"Hello," I replied, unsure of whom exactly I was speaking with.

"I head your spiritual order," the energy explained, "and we come to you in peace."

I like peace, but who's 'we'?

"We are six Pleiadian vibrations," was the reply.

Ok, I like the number six – but truly – Pleiadians?

"It has been a long time since we have spoken," it said deliberately, "but we are with you for eternity."

That's a long time.

I wondered why the head of my spiritual order didn't open Claire's eyes to look directly at me and why it didn't get up to walk around the room. If I was visiting from another planet I'd want to do that!

Then something extraordinary happened that was to silence my scepticism forever. I was suddenly overcome by a powerful magnetism, which I had felt before when I'd encountered God as a pulsating light in my bedroom. This other-world power literally touched me again. I felt it entering my body in waves through my heart. It filled my entire being with extraordinary warmth and ecstasy. I felt the immensity of unconditional love and it rendered me speechless. I simply couldn't speak. It was quite impossible to do so.

I felt compelled to close my eyelids. These and my face twitched with energy. My breathing became so deep and slow, it was quite literally out of my control. My body laboured to assimilate the enormous volume of power it was experiencing.

Tears rolled down my cheeks, uncontrollably. Had I been standing, I would surely have fallen to the ground. This pure love energy was so wondrous and real, nothing on this earth comes close to it by comparison. It was divine love. It was life giving. It was healing and it elevated me to another level of existence.

"I can feel you," I finally uttered, breathlessly, humbly. Every part of me quivered and I knew, unmistakably, that I was in the presence of a great spiritual being.

"We hoped you would," was the gentle reply. "This was our intention."

All I could do was to continue breathing deeply and slowly, laboriously, before this extraordinary presence.

"You will feel us more and more."

I'd like that very much, but how?

"We will help you with your work," was the reply, and these words reverberated within me, for some years to come.

EIGHT
INSPIRED CREATIVITY

I WENT TO THE Astor in Mount Lawley, a beautiful heritage-listed Art Deco cinema, on a Saturday afternoon. It was one of my favourite places to go. Afterwards, I returned home and felt the sudden urge to paint a picture. I hadn't painted much at all for years – just a few self-portraits and some still life.

Months earlier I had hoped that, since I was now out of university, I would find time for art again and to encourage myself, I'd purchased supplies. But since my first Light encounter I'd immersed myself in writing poetry and, as time went by, the art supplies were stashed away in my bedroom – almost forgotten about.

I began to look for the tubes of paint and finally, after much rummaging, retrieved them from a bottom drawer. I sat down on the kitchen floor with a paintbrush in hand and wondered what I was going to paint – I had no idea. The canvas board looked back at me – blankly.

I squirted out the colours red, blue, yellow and white – and gold, onto waxed paper but still, no subject came to mind. Then I noticed a light on the board, thinking nothing much about it, I put a brushstroke right there, on that illuminated spot. The light was then in another spot and I put a mark there too. I followed the light with my brushstrokes as it moved about the board. Then I heard 'the voice' again, the one from the bookstore, instructing me on how to paint the picture.

Who's that speaking to me? – I queried again.

"Go with red," it said to me. "Yes, that's right, a little more… good… now place your paintbrush a little higher up on the board… to the right. Stop there. Good. Now that's enough red paint. Don't use any more."

But I want to use more red paint.

"No more red," it said, definitely.

But I like the red, I protested.

"Go with gold," encouraged the voice, "and squirt out a lot more than you would think to use. We'll tell you when to stop squeezing."

Who is 'we'? I thought, as I cleaned the brush with turps – the smell flaring my nostrils – wiping the brush on tissues – I squeezed out some gold paint.

"More," it said. "More still. Good. Stop now."

Who exactly is that talking to me? I thought, as I followed the prompt.

The painting proceeded in this rather extraordinary way. I continued to receive clear guidance – I saw it, heard it and felt it, and I followed it.

An hour later, I felt the withdrawal of this creative energy. I was also told by the voice it was complete. I had unwittingly painted the picture upside down. I was instructed to turn it around. I looked at the image and was completely surprised by what I saw. I had painted something meaningful, yet I had done so unintentionally. Was it a mere fluke?

The image showed spiritual energy entering the top of a person's head and at their heart, then manifesting upon the earth. The swirling colours of energy in the sky and the figure standing with arms outstretched, took on the appearance of a Jesus-like figure and a flourishing tree. For me the image signified the rise of Christ consciousness in the world.

The voice also named the painting. I heard it spoken to me – *Heaven on Earth*. The following week I gave this painting to my naturopath, Dawn.

I sat before *Heaven on Earth* for hours after painting it, transfixed by its meaningful symbolism. Though it was a simple and small piece, it was very beautiful to me. I had used a lot of gold colour in the painting and it gleamed beneath the dining room lights.

I wondered about the mystifying voice that had returned to me and I wanted to understand it better. I had simply never painted in this rather automated way before. I had previously approached my art works with consideration. I had had a plan in mind.

Was this all-knowing voice my intuition? Did it originate from me or was it of another source like a spirit guide or an angel? I didn't know. I did know, however, that it was different to the usual chatter of my mind – it was clear, certain, knowledgeable, encouraging and patient.

The following day, as I sat on the couch, trying to grasp my newfound ability, the phone rang and it was my sister Mary, who was living in Sydney at the time, on the other side of the country from me.

"I had to call," she said, "to ask, if you've been painting lately?"

"*Yes*," I said – amazed to hear her mention it.

"I didn't know that!" Mary exclaimed.

"Well," I enthused, "how would you? No one does."

"Kat, my psychic friend just rang me," she explained, "and she wanted me to pass a message on to you from the angels."

"Really?" I said, staggered.

"Yes," she almost sang the message – "*Keep on with the painting!*"

"Wow – how remarkable!"

"It gets more interesting still," Mary relayed enthusiastically. "The moment I got off the phone from Kat, the phone rang again, and this time, it was my friend Brett – he then said that he had the most vivid dream about you last night, and in it you were painting really colourful art works."

"Really?" – I blurted.

"Yes… Brett says he rarely remembers his dreams but, as this one made such an impression on him, he felt he just had to share it with you."

"Blimey!" I said. "Well, what's it all about then, do you think?"

"I don't know exactly, but one thing's for sure, sister," Mary declared, "you simply *must* keep on with the painting!"

The painting, *Heaven on Earth* was not just a fluke – it was the first of many paintings created in a spontaneous inspired way. I was so full up on energy from The Light that writing and painting were natural ways in which this energy found expression. The Light quite literally generated creativity in me. From the day of my first inspired painting forward, I felt compelled to keep on with painting, and the practice powered on in my life for more than a decade – so much so that I considered it my profession for a number of years.

As I pursued the creative path, passionately, I left my previous ambition, of becoming a lawyer, well behind me – which, previous to my first Light experience, I would have considered unthinkable. Though I still liked nice things, material acquisitions and accolades mattered less and less to me, until all the meaning of my life was derived from communicating spiritual truth through writing or painting.

I went on to exhibit my inspired art works in galleries and other public spaces. I believed my paintings carried healing qualities and I was pleased to offer people a glimpse of the eternal – of transcendent scenes, spiritual entities and powerful energetic configurations.

I eventually named my painting companion – the voice – *Malachi*, simply because I liked the name. I thought it sounded grand and it felt like something grand was at play when I painted. Later, I discovered the name had a Hebrew meaning – *My angel – My messenger* – which moved me to happy tears.

Upon occasions, I felt Malachi's energy passing through me forcefully, causing my arm and hand to move with rapid automation, the muscles in my thighs to quiver and my eyelids to twitch. My breathing would become deep and slow, and I'd become entranced in the act of creating and hours passed like minutes.

The practice of surrendering to this creative force was a great therapy and education for me. I spent a lot of time interpreting the imagery and gaining further spiritual wisdom from it, meditating upon it and finding peace in the colours and patterns. I was always in awe of the undeniable connection I had with the subtle world – it was a humbling, sacred practice.

Significantly, I learnt from Malachi how to put my chattering, doubtful thoughts in the back seat and to really feel, and to act upon my feelings. I developed, over months and years, a powerful faith in the subtle communication arising from within me, and this translated into a broader trust in life.

NINE
AFRICAN WOMAN

ANOTHER EFFECT OF The Light was that I felt an urge to dance and not just any kind of dancing – *South African Zulu dancing*. Dancing ordinarily was something I avoided at all costs (like wearing bathers in public). I'd attended jazz and tap-dance classes as a child but from my teen years on, I only felt awkward and uncoordinated, and quite foolish when required to dance. It was surprising then, that I suddenly felt the need to join a dancing class, at a scout hall, in the fashionable suburb of Subiaco.

Fiki was my dance teacher. She was a voluptuous middle-aged woman with full red lips, and long tightly braided hair, and she wore colourful clothes. I thought she was beautiful. She exuded a confidence in her femininity and had no inhibitions about wiggling and jiggling all her rounded bodily bits. Her body moved with spectacular fluidity, and it was a pleasure to watch her dance. At the end of term, the class put on a performance at a popular nightspot in Fremantle and I participated with uncharacteristic enthusiasm and lack of inhibition.

As a gesture of gratitude, for all the fun I'd had, I painted Fiki an inspired painting – my fourth. Malachi named it, *A Place From Where You Come.*

When I handed it Fiki, she looked surprised.

"This is a picture of my homeland," she said smiling. "This waterfall is from where I come."

"That's its title," I mentioned, "… a place from where you come."

"How did you know to paint this?"

"It's hard to explain really," I told her, "I just know what to paint without thinking about it – it's kind of automatic."

"These, here, are spirits," she said pointing at images which I thought looked like rocks. "These spirits are very special to my people."

I was surprised to hear this – I hadn't known.

"Thank you," Fiki said, and she moved to embrace me.

Then when she moved away, something quite extraordinary happened – Fiki turned iridescent emerald green before my eyes. I was awestruck by the sight of her. Her chocolate coloured skin was now completely green. She was glowing. I stood completely still, speechless.

I thought of the glass painted African woman, hanging on my bedroom wall. I'd bought it from an open market in New Orleans, when I was a university student – I'd attended Mardi Gras.

I was suddenly transported back in my mind to when I first saw her – not in Subiaco but in New Orleans. It was afternoon when I'd stopped at a stall selling African wares. There, on the table, surrounded by wooden masks and statues, I saw a beautiful glass painting. The painting was of an African woman wearing a striking emerald-green garment. Her dark eyes appeared to be looking right at me and I instantly fell in love with her.

"How much is this painting?" I asked the stall keeper, holding the piece up for him to see.

"Sixty dollars," the man said.

I felt he was trying to take advantage of me because I was a tourist.

"I don't have sixty dollars on me," I said.

"I will not sell it for less," he said, annoyed at me. "It is an original hand painting from Africa." He then went about doing something else, so ignoring me.

I was disheartened by his unfriendliness but I wanted the painting very much. I looked at the African woman with her head shrouded, her dark face, full lips and broad nose. Her black hair was curled beneath her ears. She wore gold ornaments and berries about her hair and face, and bulbous earrings hung from her ears.

"Are you sure you won't sell me this painting for less?" I asked the stall keeper.

"No, it is sixty dollars," he said abruptly.

I reluctantly returned the painting to the table. It was very beautiful but it was too much to pay for a simple little painting.

"Ok," I said and walked away.

For the remainder of the day, I couldn't stop thinking about the painting I didn't buy. I wondered if someone else had bought it instead.

The following morning with only half an hour to go before departing New Orleans, I hurried back to the open markets, hoping the beautiful green African woman would still be there. I had resolved upon waking, that I would pay sixty American dollars for the painting, which was then the equivalent to one hundred Australian dollars. I arrived at the African wares stall and searched the table for the painting. It wasn't there. My heart sank. Someone had bought it.

Then my eye caught sight of the colour green and there it was, *the* painting but in a different position on the table from the day before. I felt so happy and relieved to see it. I reached out to claim it. It was the size of a magazine and fitted easily in my grip.

I noticed that a different man was tending the stall. I approached him cautiously.

"How much is this painting?" I asked, holding the green shrouded African woman close to my chest.

"Twenty dollars," he said.

"I'll have it," I said, perhaps a little too quickly.

As the stall keeper wrapped my painting in brown paper, I marvelled at my good fortune. I paid the twenty dollars for the painting and hurried away from the markets with my prize under arm.

The African woman in green travelled back with me to Chapel Hill and then on home to Perth. She delighted me. No one else in my life seemed to care for the painting, but I simply couldn't get enough of looking at the beautiful African woman.

Suddenly, standing before Fiki, transfixed by her magnificent transformation into a being of brilliant green light, the pieces of a rather extraordinary puzzle that had been swarming the recesses of my mind were finally coming together. Again, in flashes, I reflected back upon my unusual experiences.

Following my return from abroad, and following my encounter with The Light, I began seeing a naturopath named Agatha in Midland. She was a grey-haired, cardigan- and spectacle-wearing grandma. Nevertheless, as our relationship developed, I discovered that she was more interesting than her appearance suggested.

One morning, as Agatha led me to her consulting room, she asked, matter of factly, "Who's the African woman with you?"

"What do you mean?" I said, not knowing what she meant by it.

"I see an African woman with you," she said, as we entered her room.

There was a stream of morning light coming into the room through a large window. We sat opposite one another, at a large desk.

"In spirit," she elaborated.

"Really?" I said, surprised.

"Yes," she said, pointing at the emptiness to my left. "There."

I looked to where Agatha was gesturing, but simply couldn't see an African woman standing there.

"I can't see her," I said. Not knowing what else to add to the conversation, I remarked, "I don't know any dead Africans."

"Ok," said Agatha, and she left it at that. She then went on with my consultation and didn't mention the African woman to me again.

The same day, at midday, I visited a psychic in the hills. The psychic woman lived in a tiny house surrounded by a lot of bushland. She greeted me at the front door and walked me through her home.

"An African woman has come in with you," she said. "Do you know who she is?"

I was surprised to hear the same strange thing mentioned to me.

"I have no idea," I told the psychic. "Where is she?"

"Right here, with us, in the kitchen," she said.

We sat down at a small table. If I'd stretched out my long legs they would have gone under an old oven. I looked around but could see no African woman present. I wondered who she was, why I couldn't see her when others obviously could, and why she was following me about.

"Do *you* know who she is?" I asked.

"No, I don't," the psychic said, "but she's very connected to you."

Well you're not a very good psychic then, I thought to myself – and then hoped she couldn't read my thoughts.

Later that afternoon, I visited my chiropractor, Nicky.

"There's an African woman with you," she said. "Do you see her?"

"No!" I exclaimed, exasperated. I was lying face down on the adjustment table. I lifted my head in hope that I would finally get to see this mysterious African woman.

"I can't see her *at all*," I said, putting my face back down again. *Why don't I get to see her?*

"Do *you* know who she is?" I asked Nicky, through the opening in the table.

"Yes," she said with certainty. "She's you."

"Me? What do you mean, she's *me*?" I asked, perplexed.

"She's you from a different lifetime," Nicky explained, as she made adjustments to my spine.

"Really?" I blurted out.

"Yes, she's come to help you," she said.

"Help me with what?" I asked, as her activator clicked and clicked again.

"She wants you to 'see' like she can – she's a seer."

"How do you know all this?" I asked, unsure.

"Because she's telling me," she said matter of factly.

As I was driving home after my visit to the chiropractor, whose practice was up in the hills in the picturesque suburb of Darlington, I looked out of my car from the top of a steep decline, at the vast blue sky before me, smiled and took a deep breath. Anyone with eyes could see from this vantage point that all the white clouds in the sky had gathered together to form the one perfect image of an angel, and I felt deeply moved.

Now, at the age of twenty-three, I stood before a living African woman, whose strength and beauty I admired, and her magical appearance suddenly caused a powerful surge of recognition to arise within me. In her I could sense my own reflection and that I had once lived a meaningful life as a Zulu woman, in Africa, and her spirit was still alive in me.

TEN
MASTER TEACHER

I RECEIVED THE SACRAMENT of Confirmation at the charming Sacred Heart Church in Highgate when I was sixteen and I chose Saint Clare of Assisi to be my patron saint. I wore a candy-pink dress and fashioned a mouth full of silver braces and elastic bands.

To mark the occasion, Sister Antoinette gave me a picture of Saint Clare as a gift. I liked it a lot because it was very colourful. She told me the Saint was powerful and encouraged me to pray to her whenever I felt I needed spiritual guidance. I directed many silent prayers to Saint Clare, asking her to help me through difficult times.

Eventually my prayers to the Saint petered out. When I moved out of the family home at nineteen, I discarded the picture altogether. Then at twenty-three, I came to consider Saint Clare, once again.

It was then that I encountered the third gifted psychic healer who would have the effect of accelerating my psychological and spiritual development. Each of them had the name Clare (Claire). I feel it was the Saint who led me to them, even though I am quite sure, Sister Antoinette would not have approved of their practices.

However, it only served to strengthen my belief in the power of prayer and that help will come in ways that best serves our spiritual growth and not just our hopes or expectations.

I met the third and final Claire after the second Claire had departed my life. She also lived by the Swan River and near to the first Clare. I'd begun my inspired painting in early September. It was now late October.

Since the life review/preview and the extraordinary encounter I'd had with 'the head of my spiritual order', I felt an increasing urgency to get on with my life's work. I just wasn't sure what that was, as my future, which had been revealed to me in such a dramatic way, was now obscured from memory.

I wondered – *what did I see in the panoramic life preview that made me want to return to my physical life?*

The lack of clarity, in knowing the direction my vocation would take me, became one of my greatest challenges following university. Though I loved volunteering at a human rights organisation, and to write and paint, these weren't paying my bills.

I visited a number of psychics, hoping to discover something about my future, when really I ought to have allowed for its natural unfolding. After all, there was a reason why I couldn't recall my future in this instance. I suspect knowing it might have changed it in some way and taken away from me the personal growth that comes with making choices.

When Claire opened her front door to greet me for the first time, I was hoping to meet a talented psychic who would tell me exactly where I was headed.

"Hello, love," Claire said with a cheery English accent, "come in."

I saw a jolly, full-figured woman standing at the door.

"Hello," I said as I walked into her home, wondering why she felt familiar to me though we'd not met before.

Claire laughed and it was the same rolling laughter I had heard somewhere before.

"Did you find it alright?" she asked me with a twinkle in her eye.

"Yes thanks…" I said. Her dark hair was swept up behind her head with a clip and she wore long earrings that moved back and forth, as she moved.

"How are you?" I asked her.

"I'm great, love," she beamed. "Come on through."

Claire led me through a lounge room adjoining a kitchen, separated by a colourful curtain and it made me think of a travelling carnival. We walked to the back room of her small neat cottage.

"Sit down, love," she motioned me over to a cane chair, arranged with pillows. "Would you like a cup of tea before we start? I'm going to make myself one."

"Yes, that would be nice," I said.

"Good, love, I'll be back soon," she said with a smile.

I sat quietly in the room, looking around at all the trinkets on display and the spiritual pictures of the Buddha and Jesus hanging on the walls.

Claire returned carrying a tray with teacups and a teapot on it, and a little plastic cup filled with light-green liquid that she asked me to drink first.

"It will calm your nerves, love," she said. I hesitated – *what if she's trying to poison me*. "It's herbal," she assured me.

I drank the liquid reluctantly not wanting to appear rude and it tasted fine. I was still alive – as far as I could tell.

"How did you come to hear of me, love?" Claire asked.

"Through my naturopath Dawn, her brother has been to see you," I explained. "She said you're psychic, that you hear voices in your head like in a different language or something."

"Yes, I'm psychic, love, but I don't read fortunes," she explained. "What I do is teach people about energy."

Ok – I felt a little disappointed.

Claire put a wad of paper on her lap and held a pen. As she spoke she began to draw furiously on the top blank sheet.

"People are generally fucked, love," she said, "because they don't know who they are."

I looked at her blankly. *Did she just say fucked?*

"They are energy," she continued, "and everything is energy."

"Ok," I said (I'd heard that from Paul).

"They're so stuck up here," she pressed the pen against her head, "trying to think their way out of everything but it doesn't work because their thoughts just keep going around and around like this."

Claire showed me what she had drawn, which pretty much looked like scribble, but I got the idea it represented thought repeating on itself.

"That's what's going on inside people all day long," she pointed at the scribble.

Yes, that's me. My thoughts are definitely like a scribble.

"Do you know why it doesn't work?" she asked me. I had no idea why. "Because this is where it's at, love," she said, smacking her chest. "Truth comes from here – from your centre and not your head."

She paused to look at me intently. I didn't really get it, but I nodded anyway.

"The only way to know yourself is by letting go of all the bullshit in your life," she said. "You need to feel through your centre and develop a relationship with your breath. You are something more than all your thoughts circling around."

She went quiet and held a finger up before her nose, concentrating intently on her breathing. "This is incredibly powerful," she said, seriously.

"I would love to let go of all the bullshit in my life," I interjected.

"Well, you've come to the right place, love," she said, lowering her finger. "I give people the tools to work with so they can get more from life."

"That sounds great," I said, feeling uplifted.

"It's about being present in the here and now, love, accepting where you're at and from where you've come but knowing that you and *only you* have the power to change things – if some things aren't serving you well anymore you are the one who can create new outcomes by changing your thought patterns."

I nodded my head, accepting what she was saying – it made sense.

"It's all good, love," she smiled. "Tell me, what would you like more of in your life?"

"I want more happiness," I said, "better relationships. And I want to know what I'm supposed to be doing in this life – where I'm headed. When I was younger I had more direction and now, well… I'm confused."

"You're still young, love, you don't need to have it all worked out yet. It will come to you, at the right time, when you get in your centre," she assured me.

"I want to learn how to do that," I said.

"Don't try to work it all out," she cautioned. "The higher path is hard, love, people start on it and then stop, start, and then stop… it's not a quick fix. It takes discipline and a lifetime of effort. You'll never stop learning."

"When does life get easier?" I asked.

"The longer you do the spiritual work the easier it gets. Then the heavy shit doesn't hold you like it once did. The times you feel happy last longer until, one day, you feel at peace with yourself. I have peace now, really, love, deep peace – unshakable peace, no matter what happens in my life, but I once felt just like you do. Love, I came from real shit but I changed all that and so can you."

I knew that though I'd had many remarkable experiences in my life, there was still work to do.

"There are many levels to healing yourself, love," she affirmed. "It's like the removing of translucent onion skins. You heal – and then you arrive at the next thing – you heal that – and then you arrive at the next thing yet – and again."

I breathed deeply and nodded my head.

"And you don't have to move to India and live in an ashram like I did, love, or meditate in a cave – up a mountain, to find peace. It can happen right where you are, but it requires a lot of effort."

"I'm ready to do that," I told her.

"You'll need to change your habits, love. You'll need to become really mindful."

"Mindful… ok," I said.

"You'll need to pay attention to what you're thinking about and, in particular, what's triggering any bad feelings you have. Then remove the thought that is causing you to have that feeling and replace it with a new thought, a higher thought, so to create a better feeling in you and a better outcome."

"Ok," I said, intently.

"If you don't like your body, for instance, which is an issue for a lot of people, love, and your inner dialogue is saying, 'my body is too this, my body is too that', stop – breathe, and replace it with something neutralising like, '*I love my body*'. Saying it with feeling is powerful love – you'll need to say it for the rest of your life…"

"And if I don't believe what I'm saying?" I asked.

"It doesn't matter, love. Keep saying it anyway. Put some feeling into saying it and one day you *will* believe it."

"Will I?" I doubted.

"Absolutely, love," she smiled.

I sighed deeply – I knew I had finally met my teacher, as Paul suggested I would, my master teacher, and I was so very pleased.

Driving home from Claire's that day, my ears rang with the joyous laughter that had filled the hallway in heaven, and it dawned on me that she was my dear friend – the very same woman, who in spirit, had guided me through my life review and preview. Questions sprouted in my mind – *did Claire recall the experience too? Had she somehow orchestrated us meeting today? Or had we orchestrated our meeting?*

I was Claire's student for many years, and she was an outstanding teacher of mindfulness. It was not until a decade later that I spoke to her of my life review and preview experience – while we sat at her kitchen table, enjoying a cup of tea.

"Claire, I met you first during an out-of-body experience," I revealed. "It was a few months before we actually met here, of the flesh. There, you guided me through an elaborate life review and preview. I had the choice of remaining in spirit or returning to my physical life – obviously I chose to return to form."

"Yes, love," she said with a twinkle in her eye.

I sat with my teacup poised in my hands – eager to hear more.

"People have no idea who I truly am, love," she smiled gently and drank her tea.

ELEVEN
OUT-OF-BODY

I ASSOCIATE DULUX APPLE Green interior house-paint with some of my most memorable spontaneous out-of-body experiences. I happened to be sleeping in a small room with bright green walls. I had wanted gold-coloured walls to create a palatial ambiance but the required tins of gold paint were far too costly. The painter advised me against both my choices and suggested I go for a neutral tone, but going through a personal revolution, as I was, caused a major colour revival in me too.

After The Light encounters, my life went from conservative hues to vibrant rainbow colours. This effect was carried on through my spontaneous inspired art works.

I experienced The Light upon three occasions in my sister's bedroom at her home when she was away, working interstate. When she returned, I moved into what became the green room, which was at the end of the hallway and to the right.

I had the life review and preview out-of-body experience when my body was asleep in the green room.

The out-of-body experiences following that, I will describe in some detail. These were all green-room events, that is, my body was asleep there when my consciousness was certainly awake.

These occurred at a time when I was 'going green' between the ages of twenty-three and twenty-four, or thereabouts. It was when the glass painting of an African woman shrouded in green hung on the wall opposite my bed.

By 'going green' I mean that out of The Light experiences I grew a conscience for all living things. For instance, I began collecting house insects in glass jars, kindly taking these out to the garden rather than smacking them dead with a fly swat, as I would have done previously. I became a vegan and then a vegetarian. I was of the mind that I simply couldn't be a part of harming any life form after experiencing the intense interconnectedness of life. Being a vegan, in particular, thoroughly limited my enjoyment of eating out so I took to dining at my parents' house more frequently.

My dad never ceased in his efforts to entice me back to eating meat. He offered me a piece of cooked flesh every time I sat down to eat with him. Having a daughter who didn't eat meat conjured up war traumas for him, of lack and suffering. He pitied me. When relatives visited, and I was present, the first comment he'd always make was, "My daughter, she is a vegetarian."

"A what?" they often asked.

"No meat, she eat *no meat!*" my dad exclaimed.

Then they would all look at me, like I was inflicted with some kind of terrible illness, and proclaim their great pity for me.

Much to my sister's horror, I grew hairy armpits and dished up milk, nut and vegetable soup for dinner.

Much to my mum's horror, as if the supernatural talk and vegetarianism weren't enough, I got my nose pierced, which resulted in her shedding tears. What had become of her elegant, well-educated, ambitious Catholic daughter? The Light had altered me.

I also took to walking a lot in nature amongst trees and by the river and ocean.

I noticed the movement of ants and other insects on the

ground and along bark, the arrangement of flowers and leaves on plants, and the formation of clouds in the sky. I took a closer look at the 'smaller' things in life. I visited alternative therapists. I purified my body. I took no alcohol, no drugs, not even coffee or caffeinated tea or soda.

I attended (the third) Claire's development group weekly. From her I learnt how to meditate effectively. I meditated on the breath regularly and worked hard at changing old, habitual thought patterns that no longer served me and my expanded world-view.

It was within this transformative atmosphere that my out-of-body experiences increased in frequency. Through these also, I learnt to let go and to trust in the higher, intuitive aspect of spiritual life.

I have come to understand by the experience of rising out of form, just how very much human being's grasp at in physical life. To be separate from form, or to be out-of-body and fully conscious, is an experience of profound liberation. One feels that they have, quite literally, been let out of a cage. Life in the physical body is like a deep breath in, and life in spirit is like letting a deep breath out. It is much easier letting the breath out; it requires no effort.

All my experiences of separating from my body have been spontaneous occurrences.

The mind recalls part of an out-of-body experience, or all of it or none of it. Sometimes all I can remember is the initial separation of my spirit from form and then nothing of the journey thereafter. Other times, my sub-conscious memories surface in my paintings.

I believe the memories I do retain are not at all random but determined entirely by my higher spiritual aspect. There is value in such memories like those I shall describe, as they offer insight into the nature of the soul and greater potentialities.

Africa

The black of night was so very black and I was travelling out-of-body at a phenomenal speed. I was moving so fast that to either side of me lights streaked in lines like avenues of luminosity. What these lights were, exactly, I cannot say for sure, but I feel they may have been an effect caused by the light of my spirit.

I then arrived somewhere in Africa. I knew certainly that I was upon this ancient continent. It was either dawn or dusk as the daylight was soft, yet I was able to observe clearly a tribe of elephants before me. Dust rose from the ground as these great beasts moved slowly together.

I was now still and I lingered there, watching the elephants. It felt wonderful to be amongst the great creatures again. It felt familiar, being with them. I sensed that in some other time I had been with elephants on many occasions and that this had been my homeland. I felt that my soul had greatly benefited from a meaningful life here.

I knew that I was in spirit but still very near to the physical world. I was fully conscious. It was very clear to me that I wasn't dreaming and I felt every bit myself. I knew my cumbersome body was in bed on another continent, far away and I was so happy to be free of my body again.

It was as if I was elastic and could stretch out to the farthest destination of my soul's desire. I was also more than myself. I was Linda; yet as vast as the cosmos.

Around My Bedroom

A shocking sound woke me from my sleep. It was a ringing so loud that, had it been Earthly, it would have certainly shattered a lightbulb. If I'd heard it with human ears rather than spiritual ones, it would have ruptured my eardrums. The piercing shrill was something like feedback from an amplifier. It was something like the buzzing in the air that is heard after an electrical storm, only monstrously loud.

My heart thumped violently with fright. *Should I fight the natural urge in me to rise up in spirit?*

"Let go Linda, go with it; you are safe," I heard an assuring voice guiding me.

Who is that, I wondered? I couldn't see who was speaking, but they were close by and aware of what was happening to me. I let go of the fear and felt my spirit rise upwards. As it separated from my body, the ringing stopped.

I felt light and easy like a breeze – I floated. It was an enormous relief to be out-of-body again. I looked down and saw my physical self, lying beneath the bed covers. I had no desire *at all* to take a closer look at my face. *It's a rather spooky prospect,* I thought; though I was the spook!

I didn't feel a particular affection or disaffection for the form I had vacated because I knew it wasn't really who I am. I understood it to be a temporary guise. It is something similar to how a person feels when taking off their clothes after a working day. There is no great attachment to the piece of cloth that has been worn all day long and it is the same for the piece of flesh, left behind.

Out-of-body I felt very much like myself. I was still the same personality, with the same thoughts and feelings as I would usually have. I felt just like Linda, only lighter and without the physical discomfort I typically tolerate, due to my condition.

In mid-air I paused to consider my options. *Should I pass through the bedroom window and go and explore outside?* I wasn't sure. *What if I get lost? What if I meet other formless beings who aren't friendly? What else is moving around out there?* I didn't know. I felt reluctant to go, yet most intrigued to do so – I wanted to try out my spiritual capabilities.

Anxiety about the unknown won out. I decided to remain in my bedroom and to try out my formlessness there.

It was night but the streetlights filtered in through the closed blinds, on either side, enough to make the details of the room distinguishable. My bedroom was exactly as it should have been, in every way. There was nothing abstract, symbolic or out of the ordinary about it, though of course, my view was exceptional.

I intentionally somersaulted through the air, as I wanted to know what it felt like to do the 'astronaut thing'. I felt elated – it was so much fun. As I did this, I moved passed my stereo and heard a number of radio stations playing at once.

I then came to sit on my dresser as a way of stopping myself from floating around. I had to focus my thought to keep myself upright. There I paused for a little while. *Now what?*

I thought of my body in bed and then I was back in it again. It was instant – the thought created the effect.

Back with my body, my initial thought was – *How will I ever move this body again?* It felt incredibly heavy, like a dead weight.

Re-entering the body was easy but moving it again was not.

I focused my thoughts on moving and I slowly began to move my arm. It was quite a feat to do just that.

I moved my arms and legs and the rest of my body came to life. I got up out of bed and flicked the light on. I went over to my stereo and saw that the radio button was turned off, as it should have been. The stereo was plugged in at the electrical point and the power switch there was turned on. No music was playing.

How very extraordinary.

I Am Light

It was night and I was asleep when a powerful ringing sensation woke me. I knew what the sound meant and my mind started to panic. I was afraid, yet again, of the unknown. *What in spirit will*

I see? Where in spirit will I go? What if I encounter danger? I have stopped other 'lift-offs' before by willing it. Will I do it again?

"Let go Linda, you're ok," said a voice. "Go with it."

I let go enough and felt myself rising up again. I was out-of-body and the ringing stopped. I moved from my bedroom to the hallway and it felt so wonderful to be free again.

The house was in total darkness but as I moved along the hallway, the walls to either side of me lit up as I went – lit by the very light of my being. I was a beacon of spiritual luminosity. It was one of the most spectacular sights of my life and I marvelled at the effect I was creating.

As I approached the end of the hall, near to the dining room and kitchen, I heard a noise that startled me – I became afraid and yelled out.

"Linda, get back in your body!" a commanding voice spoke. I was back in my body immediately, with a thumping heart.

I got out of bed, flicked on the light and proceeded to flick on lights throughout the house until I reached the dining room and then the lounge room. There wasn't an intruder in sight, only Mary quietly asleep in her bedroom. I was most disappointed at myself for bringing my out-of-body experience to an abrupt end. I went back to bed – *next time I'll be more courageous.*

As I lay there, I wondered about the presence I sensed every time I left my body. To whom did the voice telling me to get back in my body belong? I heard it very clearly. Someone was watching over me, but who?

Was it the same presence I sensed when I painted my art works – that is, the director of my creativity?

Was it the same power that brought me to tears that I had felt with Claire the trance medium – 'the head of my spiritual order'?

Was it The Light I experienced that quite literally touched my heart, sending me to the highest echelon of consciousness?

Who or what was this mysterious presence I'd come to call Malachi; the presence that knew and supported me so intimately?

Was it God?

Malachi Holds My Hands

The familiar ringing sensation woke me and I rose up from my body.

"Let go," said Malachi. "Trust in the experience." And then the ringing stopped.

I became aware of a great void, blacker than black – then Malachi took hold of my spiritual hands. I felt Malachi holding them firmly, reassuringly; my hands in its hands.

Together we flew through the blackness at a moderate pace. We somersaulted and swooped. We moved like a running stream down a mountainside and through a valley, out to sea. We roamed and we soared.

I was filled with such intense glee – it was pure child's play. I felt freer than a bird in a clear blue sky and freer than the wind brushing against me lovingly as we flew.

I felt fresh and vital. It was the most magnificent joy that I can barely describe. I felt absolutely loved by Malachi. I might have even wished in my heart to have remained like this forever.

My Higher Self

"Claire," I asked, "what's the voice I hear when I'm painting?"

"It's your higher self, love," she told me.

"What does that mean exactly?" I asked.

"It's the part of you that's purely spiritual, love," she explained.

"But it sounds like someone's talking to me," I said.

"Yes, love, but it's your energy. It's the greater aspect of you."

She Was Not From Earth

I was out-of-body, awake and aware and feeling completely like myself. I was seated at a table across from a woman who was a stranger to me, though I was comfortable in her presence. We were communicating telepathically in a large meeting room like an office boardroom.

We paused to watch a man entering the room. He was in a hurry and quite preoccupied by his task at hand, for he didn't seem to notice me.

"She's from Earth," the woman said to him about me.

I was most surprised to hear her say this and in such a casual manner. *Where am I exactly and how did I get here?* I suddenly thought.

The man didn't seem to care one bit that I was from Earth. He didn't flinch at the mention of it. He didn't look at me. He said nothing. I found his manner offputting. I thought it strange that the woman's comment didn't arouse his curiosity even slightly. Was it usual for these people, who apparently were not Earthlings, though they appeared humanlike, to know of Earth and its kind? This is what they conveyed to me, by their manner.

Perhaps he can't see me. Perhaps, I'm quite simply invisible to him like air, because I'm in spirit.

"The purpose on Earth," the woman continued, looking straight at me as if she could see me quite plainly, "... is to love in form. It is the *only* place where souls can have this experience."

I was once again surprised by what was being communicated to me. *Weren't there other loving places in the universe where beings experience love in form?*

"Souls are lining up to have the experience," she assured me.

But life on Earth can be so difficult. It can be utter madness.

I was then instantly by a floor-to-ceiling window in the same room, looking out on a bustling metropolis. The room was perhaps fifteen or more storeys high. I was observing daytime activity and

I had a far-reaching view. I was astonished to see such a sophisticated society flourishing away from Earth.

In truth, it was more sophisticated than any society I have ever seen on Earth, past or present.

What I observed reminded me of an Earthly city with buildings, yet everything was different – unusual. But I can't remember how, not for the life of me. In much the same way that I cannot remember the details of my life preview, I am blocked also from remembering the details of this society. All I can recall is my feeling of experiencing it.

I watched the scene for some time because it was so fascinating to me. *Am I in heaven or am I on another planet, or is heaven on another planet?* This was my last thought, and a rather surprising thought to have. I don't recall anything after it. It was all so very, very real.

My out-of-body experiences had the effect of making me increasingly receptive to the subtle energies of spirit beings so that in my daily life, from the age of twenty-five, I began receiving messages from the dearly departed. My next personal challenge was to develop trust in after-death communications and to gather enough courage for the delicate task of delivering such messages of love to the families they were intended for.

TWELVE
DEACONESS AFTER-DEATH

I DROVE HOME ALONG a familiar route – out of the city, past boutiques and popular nightspots. It was a cool winter's afternoon – my favourite kind of day, with a pastel blue sky. I had turned the heater on in the car and the warmth soothed me. The radio played softly in the background and my mind drifted idly.

"There's a charity shop coming up on the left hand side," said a voice. "Park your car and go inside."

What a strange thought to have. Am I simply imagining this?

"There are two rooms to the shop," it said. "Go to the back room and there's something there for you. You *must* buy it."

You need to be more specific, I replied in thought, *if you expect me to believe you, otherwise it's just my mind making things up.*

"You will know when you see it," it said.

How vague. I felt annoyed at myself.

"It's coming up quickly," the voice urged me. "Be ready."

Ready for what exactly? I had absolutely no idea what shop it was referring to, and no intention of stopping anywhere along this busy stretch of road. Then something quite extraordinary happened.

"Pull over *now*," it said and some force took hold of my steering wheel, turned it and parked my car most suddenly. To my surprise this just happened to be right in front of an inconspicuous charity shop with the tiniest street frontage.

Blimey! How very bizarre and extremely unlikely. Who would believe it?

I got out of my car in dismay and looked up and down the length of Beaufort Street, which extended as far as the eye could see. Every other car bay was occupied. It was as if this particular space had been reserved especially for me. My curiosity was by now highly aroused. I could hardly wait to get inside the shop to take a closer look.

I opened the shop's door and stepped inside. It was small and cold within, and the speckled concrete floors and high ceilings reminded me of an old hospital I visited as a child. It had the same stale smell about it – of old, dusty cloth-curtains and polished wooden furniture. The windows were small and didn't let in enough air or daylight. I looked across the shop and noticed that it had two rooms, just as the voice had said. I walked by the glass counter and sparse racks of secondhand clothing, through to the back room.

I immediately walked up to a portrait, leaning against the wall on top of an old cabinet, and I touched the painting. The woman in it had beckoned me over, with her eyes. I knew for sure I had come for her. But who was she?

I peered intently at the picture. She was nobody I recognised. The painting was a metre by half a metre, painted on wooden board. It might have been the self-portrait of a hobbyist. It was not a sophisticated piece, but good enough.

The woman in the painting had dark brown shoulder-length hair, big brown eyes and pale skin. She wore a white dress that accentuated her femininity. Straps of cloth crossed over her breasts and flowed over her shoulders, like a classic bust of a Greek goddess.

Who is she? I thought.

"Pete's mum," said the voice.

What? It couldn't be?

"Yes, it's me," the voice replied.

Is my friend's dead mother speaking with me?

"Yes. I am," she said.

Blimey. I can hardly believe it.

"Believe me. It's true," she said.

I had, months before, met Pete through a mutual friend. He was very likeable. He thought deeply about matters and was passionate about the environment. His mother, who had been dear to him, died five years earlier of multiple myeloma (tumours in the bone marrow), aged sixty-two.

I knew little about her. Pete had only mentioned his mum to me briefly. I'd never given her any thought, other than that. I didn't even know her name. What I did know was that, in life, she had been one of Australia's first women priests, a Presbyterian deaconess.

"Yes, you really are speaking with me," she kept reassuring me, but I wasn't entirely convinced. I had never had an experience like this before. Yes, I'd heard 'the voice' but not a voice belonging to a friend's dead mother.

"Take the painting home and make changes to it," she said matter of factly. "I've got different coloured eyes from the woman in the painting. Mine are bright blue like my son's. Please give him the painting. It will be very meaningful to him."

I almost choked on her suggestion. I would be seeing Pete in a few days and I hadn't seen him for months, though we spoke on the phone more frequently. He lived in the country and I had business to attend to there. *I can't possibly give this painting to Pete,*

I protested. *What ever would he think of me? What if it isn't really you? What if it upsets him?*

I delivered the painting to the front counter and paid twenty dollars for it. I left the shop and walked out onto the footpath holding the painting under my arm. The air was brisk and I hurried to the car. *I'll think on the painting as I'm driving.* I enclosed it in the boot and drove on to my parent's house, to the art studio I had there. It was a change of my afternoon plans.

My mum's home office (my mum was now retired), which was the scene of my very first supernatural experience at age sixteen, was now my dedicated studio space. I created inspired paintings there and I had been working towards exhibiting my pieces in a number of country galleries.

When I arrived at my studio, I went inside and sat on the floor with the painting of Pete's mum laid down before me. I bent over it and scrutinised it closely. I then proceeded to make changes to it, pausing every so often to look at it again, all the while hearing clear instructions from the voice that belonged to the spirit of Pete's mum.

"Change the brown eyes to blue eyes," she said.

"Are you sure?" I asked.

"Yes, Pete has my eyes," she told me again.

Geez, I hope so. Pete's were the bluest eyes ever, bluer even than Paul the alchemist's. I mixed a brilliant blue hue and carefully applied it over the brown eyes already there. I paused to look at her iridescent eyes. Pete's mum looked back at me more intently than before.

"You've got lovely eyes," I said.

"Thank you," she replied. "Next paint a chain and crucifix around my neck." I did exactly as she suggested. Then I felt a strong urge to paint a segment of armour on her left upper arm. "On the armour, paint a blue bird."

"Why, a blue bird?" I asked, but there was no reply. *How*

unusual. I reluctantly painted a blue bird on the armlet, the same hue as her eyes.

"That's all," she said, precisely. I made no further alterations to the painting.

"Please give my son this painting of me," she said again, "it will mean so much to him. Tell him that mum is with him still and loves him."

I was in two minds about sharing any of this with Pete and, in the time leading up to my departure, I felt anxiety about it. She obviously knew I had my doubts and championed her cause for days.

The day soon arrived when I packed up the boot of my car and I almost didn't take the painting with me. It was a last-minute decision to put it in the boot on top of my luggage and to conceal it completely with a towel. I still didn't know if I would give it to Pete, once I was in his company.

For the entire three-hour journey south, my mind kept returning to the painting in the boot and what I would do with it – and I was distracted by Pete's mum 'gnawing' in my spiritual ear.

When my car tyres crunched over the rust-coloured, pebbled driveway at Pete's rural coastal home in Prevelly, he promptly appeared outside to greet me. I was pleased to see my friend again, but I was also nervous about him seeing inside the boot of my car. We always shared an honest rapport, but was Pete ready to hear that I'd been speaking with his dead mother? Was I ready for the consequences?

I got out of the driver's seat and opened the boot to retrieve my travel bag. I did this hurriedly, so Pete wouldn't see the painting hidden beneath the towel. He didn't see it and in his gentlemanly way insisted on carrying my bag inside the house.

"It's so nice to be here," I chirped, admiring the country views from the lounge room. We soon settled in by a fire with piping hot cups of herbal tea and enjoyed a long conversation in the comfort of the armchairs. Then our talk turned to my paintings, which I'd come to the country to find support for, and I cautiously began to reveal my secret to him.

"I have something to show you," I said, a little anxiously.

"What is it?" Pete asked.

"It's a painting," I told him, "but it's different from my usual ones."

"I want to see it," he enthused.

"It's not really *my* painting," I explained. "It's a painting someone else did and I found in a charity shop… actually I was… led to it… but I've made a few changes to it… there's quite a story behind it… and… should I just get it?"

"Yes," he said, "where is it?"

"It's in the boot of my car," I said, getting up.

"Would you like me to get it?" he offered.

"No… no that's ok," I said quickly. "I'll do it."

I promptly left the lounge room with Pete sitting there looking after me, as I hurried outside to retrieve the painting. I opened the boot and tossed the towel aside, exposing Pete's mum to the cool air. Her bright blue eyes looked straight at me.

This better not be a big mistake, lady, I warned her. But she remained silent.

Without another thought about it, I took courage, closed the boot and carried the painting into the house. Pete was there waiting, sitting as I had left him. I placed the painting nearby on the floor, leaning it against a piece of furniture, and I stood in front of it so he couldn't see it. I wasn't quite ready for the grand moment of truth.

"Ready?" I sighed. Pete nodded. Then I moved aside so he could see it.

I watched him look over it without any change of expression to his face. My heart sank. I looked at the painting and then back at him. *Oh dear, I've really got it wrong. I shouldn't have believed in that bloody voice in my head.*

"Does she remind you of *anyone*," I asked, pausing, "like… maybe… your mum?"

It was like a switch going on. Pete's face immediately lit up.

"*Yes!*" he exclaimed. "But when she was younger – wow, that's amazing!"

"Really?" I queried.

"Yes, it's *really* her! Wow!" he said, stunned, staring at the painting. "When you said, 'does she remind you of anyone?' I thought you meant someone alive, now, someone that we both know… that's *definitely* my mum when she was about thirty years old."

"I feel relieved," I explained. "I doubted myself. I almost didn't give you the painting."

"I'm so glad you did," he beamed, still staring at the painting.

Then I proceeded to tell him how I came to find it and how I was inspired to make changes to it, by the spirit of his mother.

"I have a photo of mum that is just like this painting," Pete said suddenly, getting up from his armchair with a charge of energy. "It's almost identical. Mum's wearing the same white dress in the photo. I hope I can find it for you."

"That would be incredible to see," I said.

As he crossed the room and went up the stairs, I called after him.

"And did she have blue eyes?"

"Yes… like mine," he called back.

Pete was gone for ten minutes and all the while I looked at the painting thinking I ought to trust in my sensitivities more.

When he returned, he held in his hand the much anticipated photograph of his deceased mother as a younger woman. He passed it to me so I could take a closer look. It was the first time I'd ever seen a photograph of her.

"That's incredible!" I agreed. "It *is* just like the painting but in black and white. Even the hair is styled the same."

"I told you," he smiled, pleased.

"Your mum's amazing, Pete," I said.

"I can feel her here with us now," he said, delighted.

"Me too," I agreed.

I described to Pete how I'd felt the spirit of his mum with me for days, and how she'd insisted again and again that I give him the painting.

"The crucifix obviously symbolises her faith but what do you make of the blue bird?" I asked, perplexed.

"She *loved* blue birds," Pete explained. "It was her favourite creature of all. She wore a blue bird pendant on a necklace."

"Really?" I exclaimed. "That's truly remarkable… and the armour, no doubt, shows her strength of spirit."

"Yes, mum was a strong personality and her spirituality meant a great deal to her."

"She still is a strong personality," I said – and we laughed.

"This is really special," Pete spoke softly, clearly moved. "Thank you."

"I'm so glad it all means something to you. And I'm hearing your mum – she wants me to tell you something."

"Ok," he said.

"She says she is often with you. She wants you to have the painting as proof of her spiritual survival."

"I do feel her from time to time," Pete acknowledged.

"She loves you," I said, feeling a rise of emotion in me. "She has *so* much love for you Pete."

My friend gently nodded his head.

"She's really proud of you too," I continued to relay his mum's communication. "She's proud of the man you are and of the man you will become. She supports the decisions you will make. And it's all going to be ok."

"Thanks," Pete said softly. "It's amazing that she's come to me through you."

"I know," I chuckled, "I *never* expected this."

I quietly thanked Pete's mum for trusting me and for making me a part of this very meaningful love connection with her son.

The following day, Pete and I went for a long drive further south, to the beautiful coastal town of Denmark to which I'd never been. It took us three hours of driving to get there. The route was really picturesque and we both fell into an easy, contemplative silence. The road wound through native forest and was illuminated by shafts of light which created the effect of a natural cathedral.

We were feeling hungry by the time we arrived at our destination in the mid-afternoon and decided to find a place to eat. Pete parked the car and then we got out and stretched our legs. We walked through the township looking for a bakery or café. None of the places we went into were serving lunch.

Then we came upon a rather plain looking café. Its most remarkable feature was that it served lunch at 2:30 in the afternoon. It was clean and devoid of patrons. We looked for a table to sit at and noticed a sign with an arrow pointing to a courtyard out the back.

We walked out the back door of the café and into a small courtyard, where we chose a table alongside other patrons. Plants grew in pots and in a small garden bed nearby. It was not a particularly beautiful garden but the plants, at least, were alive.

We began to look over the menus, when we were surprised by a little blue bird that flew right by us at a great speed.

"Look at that bird!" I said, astonished. I'd never seen anything like it before, in all my life. It was the bluest bird ever – it looked utterly magical.

"It's a Blue Wren," Pete said. "They're native to this area."

"It's iridescent," I said. "It looks like a creature straight out of heaven."

"It makes me think of mum," Pete said and I agreed.

We watched the delicate little blue bird flutter about joyfully. It flew from a plant to a chair to our table. It paused so we could admire it and just as quickly it departed, over our heads, for another chair at a different table. Then it darted off once more for a plant in the garden.

Then, there suddenly appeared so many blue birds that we quickly lost count. It was such an extraordinary spectacle, yet no one other than us seemed to take notice of it. We were quite literally encircled in a fluttering of delightful blue birds, right until our meals arrived at the table. Then the birds all disappeared and we didn't see them again.

"Mum really wants us to know that she's around," Pete laughed.

"Her spirit is amazing," I said.

After lunch we returned to Pete's car, a different way from the way we'd come in. We walked straight out from the café so that we were directly opposite its frontage. For no particular reason, we both turned back to look at the café we'd just left, at exactly the same time. And, as we did, we saw for the first time the café's signage high up on its roof: *The Blue Wren Café*.

"Wow!" we exclaimed in unison and burst out laughing. It made such an impression on us. There was no question in our minds that we had been led to this little café by Pete's mum so we could experience her spiritual magic. We had unwittingly chosen to dine at a café devoted to the blue bird, his mum's signature creature. We had driven hours for this soulful connection.

It made me realise to what great lengths love will go to fulfil itself, in this life and the afterlife.

THIRTEEN
MAY TRANSITIONING

MAY WAS THE colour of autumn leaves, but her nature was summer. She was active, ordered and warm. Her first name was Delilah but as an adult she went by her second name only – it suited her. To me, she was Aunty May but she was actually not my aunty, but I would very much have liked it if she had been.

Aunty May was my next door neighbour from the first day I entered this world to the day I moved out of my parent's home, as a young woman of nineteen. It is only now, as I approach mid-life, that I deeply appreciate her nurturing and stabilising influence on my childhood. She created a very calm environment in which I could relax, let down my guard and allow my childish imagination to play. I spent a lot of time at Aunty May's house. She looked after me when my parents worked and her son Craig was my very best friend.

Craig and I were the same age. We went to the same kindergarten, primary and secondary schools and we enjoyed many happy times together. He was the first boy I kissed. He was my first childhood sleepover friend – we drank milk and ate cold orange-marmalade toast together as Kenny Rogers and Dolly Parton played on the turntable. We played nurses and doctors behind the back shed. We raised tadpoles into frogs. We climbed trees, until Craig fell off his perch and broke his arm. We explored our neighbourhood on bike and foot. It was the quintessential childhood friendship.

"I'm going to marry Craig, one day," I told Aunty May matter of factly when I was five. My heartfelt declaration over the backyard fence made her and my mum smile.

Aunty May was a school teacher and a champion athlete. She had a special way about her – when she spoke, it was directly to me in a soft, friendly tone. She waited patiently to hear my reply.

If this wasn't wonderful enough she also made purple pikelets and her biscuit jar was full of pink, iced biscuits with hundreds and thousands… my favourites!

It was Aunty May who took me to my first day of kindergarten because my parents had to work. She encouraged me when I felt overwhelmed by the unfamiliar surroundings. It was she who waved to me during school assemblies and watched me run and lose my races at school carnivals – my parents were absent as they worked.

When we turned seven, Craig got a brand new, shiny brother with white blonde hair. I had been hoping for a baby girl but when I saw Stewart's lovely little face for the first time, I fell in love with him instantly. I promptly named him 'Stewie' and he soon became my favourite plaything. Once he could crawl and then walk, Stewie followed me about in a singlet and nappy.

Craig, however, wasn't so pleased with our new attachment, as Stewie had a way of getting in the way of a good game of cricket.

By the time we were thirteen, the hormones kicked in and Craig and I rapidly went our separate ways. I became overly consumed with my studies and my awkwardness, and a lifetime of friendship became unstuck.

By our twenties, Craig and I were virtual strangers to one another. I no longer played with Stewie. At best I watched him grow up from our dining room window, as he crossed over our front lawn each day on his way home from school.

I no longer spent time talking with Aunty May. We exchanged a friendly, yet simple, greeting from time to time.

Then she became sick with cancer. I was twenty-six years old and soon to be married to Robert. Little did I know then, that this was to be the start of a unique bond between Aunty May and I. Furthermore, little did I know then, that one of the most emotional memories of my life would involve her.

Why did she get cancer? I thought. It didn't seem fair. Not that it's fair for anyone to suffer ill health, but Aunty May least of all. She had always cared for herself – she had an enviable physique, was fit and energetic, capable, sociable and kind-hearted, and appeared to have good balance in her life.

We were all very upset at the news, my parents and sister alike. My parents regularly spoke to Aunty May's husband, Roger, about how her treatment was progressing. My mum helped out occasionally by cooking a meal for them.

Then about half-way through Aunty May's illness, I began to dream of her. In these dreams she would tell me how she was keeping. At one point, she was doing better.

I soon came to realise that these dreams weren't dreams at all in the usual sense, when my mum would relay to me what Uncle Roger had said, and it echoed what I knew already about Aunty May, as she had already told me in the 'dreams'. Rather, I was having visitations from her in spirit – that is, our spirits were speaking in the night as our bodies slept.

I was so moved by the soul communication we shared that I created a painting for Aunty May. The image that came forth was that of the divine light and it illustrated the journey the soul takes when transitioning from the physical to the spiritual reality.

I never gave Aunty May the painting, which is a regret of mine. But then I found it all too confronting. I had not spoken to Aunty May face-to-face, 'of the flesh', for a decade and a half. Would my sudden appearance at her bedside signal to her that I believed she was going to die? If I shared with her my spiritual encounters, might she think I was mad? Rather, we continued to meet at night on the spiritual plane, until my wedding day.

❧

I knew I would marry Robert from the first time I laid eyes on him. I had accompanied Mary to her friend's house for a barbeque. Rob arrived there late, carrying a tray of baked chicken pieces and though I was a vegetarian, I was thunderstruck. A powerful sense of destiny arose within me – I just knew he was *'the one'*.

Rob was older and taller than me and extremely handsome, and I wondered how I would ever come to utter a word to him, let alone allow him close enough to me to know all of my imperfections.

That night, I didn't say one word to him and I barely had the courage to look his way.

It was three years later that he asked me out on a date and I accepted happily (I was twenty-five). I was out of my comfort zone but I had been steadily moving towards this shift in my personal life – through all the inner-work I'd been doing with Claire.

On our first date, my husband-to-be kissed me passionately in the falling summer rain outside a fish factory, at the historic port of Fremantle. It was to seal our fate.

All the healing I had received in my life, up to the point of entering into a relationship with Rob, enabled me to allow my heart's longing to manifest. That longing, which I believe is everyone's longing, is to be bonded to another in love.

Before The Light, it was almost too painful to believe that someone so wonderful could love me.

Without Rob, my head might have remained too much in the

clouds. With him, I discovered the middle road, a way to live happily amidst the spiritual and physical realities, simultaneously.

All that chanting of, 'I love my body', culminated in a shift in my body image. I even suggested to my fiancé that we have nude pictures taken by a photographer in town, something that in the past I would never have done – and he obliged me. Upon this occasion I felt at ease beneath the warm spot lights. We laughed as we struck our poses to the upbeat tunes of gypsy folk music blaring from the studio speakers.

Who would have thought such a thing likely when for so many years I'd gone to great lengths to conceal my loathsome body? Having the black and white photographs to reflect upon, I realised what progress could be made in a relatively short period of time. I was changed. Though I was still disfigured, what I saw of the photographs was beauty. I was more beautiful than I had ever before allowed for.

My parents fell in love with Rob because he consumed all the food they laid out before him, which in their culture is a very good thing.

"Robert is a very good eater," my dad chirped.

He also showed a genuine interest in them and their culture.

"Robert, is so calm, so nice, I couldn't love him more if I'd given birth to him myself," my mum chirped.

Furthermore, my dad believed it was due to Rob's influence that I reverted to being an omnivore, which was not entirely true – rather I'd become very iron deficient despite my best efforts to stay healthy.

One evening, dad's eyes bulged with disbelief when I ate a prawn.

"Oh thank you Robert!" he burst with joy, shaking Rob's hand vigorously.

When I ate a piece of chicken, dad shed a tear. It was then, perhaps, that Rob first realised he had come into a rather emotional family.

Our wedding day was a wonderful affair with family and friends in attendance – I was a few months short of turning twenty-seven.

As tradition would have it, I spent the eve of our wedding day at my parent's home.

By early afternoon, I'd been transformed into a modern-day Cinderella going to the ball.

When the Daimler arrived in the driveway, the neighbours flocked to their front lawns to catch a glimpse of the glamorous procession. As we descended the verandah stairs of our family home, I saw Aunty May waiting patiently on her front lawn, to see me too. It rather took me by surprise and I felt a well of emotion rise in me. There she stood in her candy pink dressing gown, her strawberry blonde hair neatly brushed, leaning on her crutches, for the opportunity to admire me on my wedding day.

"Hello Aunty May," I said, waving my long manicured fingers at her.

My heart felt like it was going to burst at its seams, seeing the effort she had made for me. She smiled at me and I smiled back. I wondered what she might be thinking. I felt ashamed that I hadn't yet taken a courage pill and made the effort to visit her in her obvious ill health. I felt my jewel clad ears turn bright red.

I looked around to see other neighbours admiring me, some I had known all my life. I waved at them like a starlet and then stepped into the Daimler, gathering up the skirt of my exquisite dress. I sat close to my dad who was beaming in his black tuxedo. He was like a beacon radiating fulfilment.

"I am so proud!" he exclaimed.

He deserved to feel such joy and my heart expanded with happiness for being the cause of such delight in him.

The Daimler backed out of the driveway and drove on down the street as people waved and cars tooted their horns, in celebration.

I looked back at Aunty May, who was still standing on her front lawn watching the Daimler drive away, with a smile on her lips.

✺

I woke with a start. It was as if someone had punched me in the chest. There was no physical sensation to it but the impact was still breathtaking. The bedroom was dark and my husband was asleep next to me. I had just dreamt of Aunty May. I knew it was a soul communication rather than a mere dream. She had just been to visit me again in spirit.

The scene had been of a beautiful sunny day. I was in my front yard tending to plants in the garden bed by the neighbouring fence which was sheltered by the carport. Aunty May's head appeared over the fence. I looked up to see her looking straight at me.

"I'm feeling much better now," she said – then I jolted awake.

When I settled myself, I hoped, pulling my bedclothes up around my head, maybe Aunty May is finally on the mend – and I went back to sleep.

In the morning when the sun was up, I mentioned the experience to Rob.

"I think Aunty May's going to get better from here on," I said smiling.

The following night, I found it difficult to fall asleep, for no particular reason. I tossed and turned and my mind ticked over. When I last looked at the alarm clock, it was exactly 2 am – then I woke with a start.

Aunty May had been to visit me again.

"I'm totally healed now," she said, smiling at me – she looked absolutely radiant.

In the morning, I told Rob that Aunty May had visited me again in the night.

"She looked really good," I said. "And she told me that she's been healed. I just know she's going to beat the cancer now."

At work that day, the phone rang – it was 9:30 am.

"Good morning, how can I help you?" I chirped.

"Linda?" spoke my dad's distinct voice.

"Hi dad," I said – wondering why he was calling me at work.

"My daughter, I have bad news…" he said solemnly, "May die – last night."

"Oh no," I said, shocked.

"I am *so* sad," he said, "she be very nice lady. Not bad word between us in thirty years."

"What time did she die?" I asked him – recalling my vision.

"I don't know," he said, "ask your mum – she know."

Later, when I spoke to my mum, I asked her the same question.

"What time did Aunty May die?" I asked her.

"It was two o'clock in the morning," she said. "It was then that we heard Roger open the metre box and turn the sprinklers on."

FOURTEEN
SIGNS OF SURVIVAL

"CUT SOME OF these roses and make a bunch for Roger," Aunty May said to me. "Please, give them to him, and tell him that I love him."

I woke with a start and caught my breath in the darkness – she had been to visit me again.

In this communication, it was the scene of another perfect sunny day. Aunty May looked as she did when I was a child. She moved easily and looked healthy – there were no crutches anymore. She acknowledged my presence, as she always did, by looking directly at me and speaking directly to me.

She led me to the garden next to her bedroom window. The same garden I looked into as a child from my bedroom window, as our house was elevated. It was the same garden in which Craig and I played with toy cars and trucks as children, making roads in the dirt. It had grown into a beautiful rose garden with towering stems that sought out the sunlight. From it Aunty May created beautiful displays for her vases. Specifically, it was *her* rose garden but I wasn't to discover this until years later. Uncle Roger too had a rose garden but in a different place in the backyard. She wanted me to make a bouquet of her roses for her beloved husband.

I felt a great responsibility to fulfil Aunty May's wishes, though I had no idea how I was going to go about it. What would Uncle Roger think of me as a grown woman, jumping over the fence, cutting Aunty May's roses and turning up at his door, roses in hand, saying they were a gesture of love from his recently deceased wife? The thought of one of a number of reactions from him, none of them pleasant, filled me with dread, so I opted for doing and saying nothing. I felt regret for my cowardice – I felt I had let the dear lady in spirit down, as I felt I had before she died. I knew she wanted me to let her husband know, in his deep feelings of losing her, that she was not lost to him in spirit.

She wanted him to know, "I am alive, I am myself, I am with you and I still love you, as I always have." Unfortunately, I couldn't bring myself to the task of relaying this sentiment to Uncle Roger who I believed was a complete non-believer in spiritual reality.

"I want you to get a book for Roger," she told me one morning, soon after.

I was taking a shower and now I could hear her in between my thoughts. *Am I imagining that you're talking to me?* I asked Aunty May.

"It really is me," was the reply.

It carried on in this vein for the duration of the shower. *How can I know for sure that it's you and not just my imagination?* I felt challenged, yet again, by the voice within.

If you really want me to do this for you, I finally said in thought, *you've got to give me a sign that shows me that I'm really talking to you and not just making it up. I don't know what exactly but make it really obvious, so I can't mistake it as anything else. I'm not getting any book unless I get an almighty sign, one that absolutely knocks my socks off!*

Following the shower, I dressed and Rob and I drove to our local shopping centre for a few food items and the weekend newspaper.

"I just want to have a quick look at the bookstore," I told him.

"Ok," he said, "we'll meet back here, at the supermarket."

I hadn't mentioned the episode in the shower to him because I wasn't entirely sure about it. He entered the supermarket and I walked on a little further to the bookstore.

In the bookstore, I stood before the Spirituality/Self-Help section scanning the shelves for the book I had in mind for Uncle Roger. It was *The Eagle and the Rose* by Rosemary Altea, an acclaimed medium, describing her remarkable experiences with the spirit realm. Eventually I saw the book there and made a mental note of it. I then left without buying it; I was still waiting for a definite sign. *Perhaps Aunty May wants her husband to visit a medium,* I pondered.

Though I had not lingered in the bookstore for long, Rob was already at the checkout with a trolley full of the food items when I met up with him. He was placing the food on the counter. I excused myself as I squeezed past three young adults, who were waiting next in line.

"Did you find what you were looking for," Rob asked me.

"Yes," I said, but I didn't elaborate.

As I waited, I looked around the supermarket and caught the eye of one of the young men who was waiting next at our checkout. He was casually talking and laughing with his other two companions, a male and a female, but at the same time he was looking at me.

I didn't think anything much of it at first. I looked back at Rob and the checkout operator to see what kind of progress we were making. As groceries passed along from the counter and into plastic bags, I looked about again. I couldn't help but notice yet again that the same young man was looking at me a little too intently. I thought, *Maybe he's checking me out. But he's being a bit too obvious about it.*

It was getting a bit uncomfortable so I decided to look straight back at him, expecting him to look away, but he simply looked right back at me, and smiled, in a way that was too familiar. *Maybe he mistakenly thinks he knows me from somewhere.*

"Linda?" he said.

How does he know my name? Then I could hardly believe it! "*Stewie...?*" I uttered, totally shocked.

"I haven't been called that in the longest time," he said, smiling.

"*Oh my God!*" I exclaimed – my heart swelling with emotion. "You're so grown up. When did that happen?"

Stewie and his friends simply laughed but I was serious – when *did* it happen?

"This is Stewie, Aunty May's youngest boy," I blurted out to Rob. "We grew up together."

"Hello," Rob said.

"Hi," Stewie smiled at him.

"I'm married now," I said, pointing at Rob.

"Yes, I know," Stewie said. Then there followed an awkward pause.

"Sorry about your mum," I said, regretfully.

"It's ok," he said. "Thanks for all the lovely things your family said about mum in the paper. It was really nice."

The glands in my neck were now starting to swell with the emotion flooding out from my heart. I thought it was best to change the subject before I started crying in the supermarket.

"Stewie was the cutest little baby," I said to everyone listening. "He used to follow me around everywhere – we were so fond of each other."

"How long has it been?" Stewie asked.

"I haven't seen you for at least five years or more," I said. "And look at you now – you're a spunky man."

We all laughed at this, as Rob moved the trolley forward. Our time at the checkout was over.

"Good to see you, Stewie," I said, thoughtfully.

"Yes... " he smiled, "... bye."

His friends smiled. Rob smiled. But I just felt like I was going to cry my eyes out. I swallowed the emotion. I really wanted to give Stewie a hug and to take away the pain he must have been feeling but, regrettably, I just walked away.

All the way back to our car my thoughts were spinning around in my head. *What were the chances of bumping into Stewie like that? How did the spirit of Aunty May get our paths to cross like that? Magic certainly is in the timing.* It was the sign I'd been waiting for and it would certainly have knocked my socks off, had I been wearing any. I was yet again totally blown away by the power of spirit. I had experienced it with Pete's mum and now I was experiencing it with Stewie's mum too. I felt so blessed.

A few days after our unlikely supermarket encounter, I was crying with my dad in a crowded crematorium to farewell Aunty May. The tears finally came pouring out – it was a flood. I'm not immune to feeling the physical loss of a loved one. I felt for Aunty May's family who had been through so much in recent months and who had hoped with all their hearts that she would recover from the cancer that ravaged her body.

I was sad that I had never told her before she died just how much she had meant to me as a child. I was sad I hadn't had the courage to tell her about heaven and the loving light of Spirit – it might have meant something to her. I was fed up with my logical mind that often sought ways to discredit my heart's knowing. Surely life would be easier in some ways if I could simply believe in nothing other than the tangible, but I knew there was more to life than this.

At the close of the service, Aunty May's favourite song played over the speakers. It took me right back to my childhood and I cried my eyes out.

After the service I hugged her children. It wasn't so long ago that we had laughed and played together.

A few days later, I returned to the bookstore and purchased the book Aunty May wanted Uncle Roger to have. But in one last awkward moment I chose not to mail it to him. Rather, I mailed it to Craig – I don't know what he ever thought of it. I was still concerned by 'what the neighbours might think'.

It was something that weighed heavily upon my heart and mind – I had not fulfilled Aunty May's wish. I had not delivered the book to Uncle Roger.

Since her passing, every time I visited my parents, I would pause in their driveway to contemplate whether or not I'd knock on Uncle Roger's door on that day. Not today, I'd say to myself, for some reason or other.

But one day, I did knock on Uncle Roger's door and he opened it with a smile.

"Hi," he said, warmly, "come in."

"Hello," I said, stepping inside.

I hadn't been inside their home for many years but it was as I remembered it to be. I stood in the meals area, next to the kitchen and the past washed over me. I almost expected to see Aunty May, standing by the counter with a lovely smile.

But on this day, Uncle Roger was at home alone. I felt a little anxious and perhaps he could tell.

"I would like to tell you about some of the experiences I've had with May's spirit," I began, "… but I don't want to upset you."

"That's fine," he said. "Come into the family room."

We walked into the TV room, which is where Craig and I used to play Lego together – we'd construct great towns and space stations.

"I've wanted to talk to you for a while," I admitted, "but I didn't quite know how to go about it."

"Sit down," he gestured, calmly.

I looked at the brightly coloured sofas in the room and was instantly transported back in time. I sat in an armchair and Uncle

Roger sat in another, across from me. From there I looked across the room and saw a large family portrait framed, resting against a sofa – it was relatively recent.

I felt the spirit of Aunty May in the room with us – and it brought me comfort to see her picture looking back at me. Uncle Roger looked at me with quiet anticipation.

"I've had lots of dreams about her," I said, "but they were more than dreams really… visitations."

I wondered if he was thinking I was mad already. There was a pause and my eyes darted between the family portrait and Uncle Roger.

"I feel nervous," I said. "You don't really believe in the spiritual, do you?"

"It's ok," he encouraged. "I'm not closed to it."

"Ok," I said, relieved, "that makes it easier for me."

I continued with greater ease as I described to him my varied experiences involving his wife – I also mentioned the book she wanted him to read.

I don't know what Uncle Roger made of it all, or if he ever bought and read the book, but he listened patiently, and I was pleased that I had finally grown the courage within myself to share these meaningful experiences with him.

"Some other people who knew May have told me they've dreamt of her too since her passing," he said, "but I haven't had any dreams about her yet."

He kind of chuckled when he said this, but there was little doubt in my mind that Uncle Roger wished it was he who was 'dreaming' of his dear wife. For whatever reason, he could not sense her, but others could, and in this way she was reaching out to reassure him, of her enduring love and spiritual survival.

FIFTEEN
REVELATIONS

AS A CHILD, I had always manoeuvred around the topic of war very carefully.

"Dad, what was war like?" I asked.

"Very bad," he'd state briefly. "They kill my father and my brother and beat my mother. We cry very, very much."

There was never much more that he elaborated on. He was a man of few words and was always busy doing things. He'd be off and out of sight before I had another chance to probe. I always felt disappointment. I so very much wanted to understand him better.

My sister poked and prodded but it never amounted to much either. Sometimes we'd ask our mum to explain the war to us and she went a little deeper.

"During the war, your father was always hungry," she would say as the iron steamed and hissed, as she pressed on with her Sunday afternoon chore.

"There was never enough food," she continued. "Can you imagine how hard it was for your Baba Mara, the poor woman, to know that her children were suffering?"

Dad was a great fan of Westerns, however, he never watched a war film on television.

"I already know about war," he'd retort. "I was there." Then he would get up from his armchair and go to bed.

Mary and I watched war movies together, bleary eyed. We watched those harrowing movies so we could understand our family better.

><

A couple of years following Aunty May's passing my father became gravely ill. He had been enjoying his retirement when suddenly and dramatically his fortunes turned. I was at my home on a Sunday afternoon when I received a phone call from a relative informing me that my dad had been admitted to emergency at the city hospital.

I raced to the Royal Perth and found him lying on a bed surrounded by medical staff and he was the colour grey. I was told immediately by doctors that his condition was very serious. Remarkably his aorta had split from his heart to his kidney. I thought, *This time he will surely die.*

The volume of grief I felt overwhelmed me. The situation brought forth primal emotions of attachment I never knew I possessed. The life and times I'd spent as his daughter raced through my mind. I was most upset that he might never meet my (yet to be born) children. He had long wished to be a Dida (grandfather).

Dad was rushed into surgery and he was stitched back together by some very clever doctors. However one of his kidneys was completely defunct and the other functioned at less than half of its capacity. Also he was riddled with aneurisms and his demise appeared imminent.

We visited dad in the intensive care unit the day following his lifesaving surgery. It allowed me to experience a condition commonly called ICU psychosis. It played out with great drama as his mind reacted adversely to the drugs being administered and to the physical trauma he was going through. He became paranoid and agitated, regressing into wartime memories, as if he was reliving his past in the present time. He believed the doctors and nurses caring for him were enemy militants intending to murder him, and that he was not in a hospital but in a prisoner of war camp. He implored mum and me to leave; otherwise we would suffer a similar fate.

It was very sad to glimpse the psychological trauma he suffered through as a child, yet also revealing and it left me with a greater understanding of the grief I had felt festering in our family, all of my life.

A couple of days later, dad was back to his usual cooperative and friendly manner – enjoying the attention of the female nurses.

"I am not afraid to die," he declared, resolute and buoyant, as I sat by his bedside. "Do not be sad when I go. When I be younger man, yes, sometimes I worry to die. But now I see my two beautiful daughters grow up, they marry and, oh, I am *very, very happy*!"

As he recuperated at home, dad and I sat out on the verandah in the sunshine one afternoon and he spoke intimately with me for the first time, about his early life trauma. This was a remarkable shift in our relationship as he had always previously avoided sharing his story. The little boy poured out of him and I listened keenly, lapping up the rare insight on offer.

"Ivan – he be my father and your Dida. He be *glavar* – a village leader – like a mayor. They kill him because he be glavar. But he not be fighter. He be very good man – smart, hard-worker, kind to everybody – everyone like him and my mother.

Mara, she be very good woman – very good cook and she deliver the babies – she deliver the babies all around villages. She be mother of seven children – five boys and two girls and I be youngest. She love me very much.

Together, my father and my mother grow grapes, figs, cherries, almonds and walnuts – plenty. Big cherries like golf balls. Oh you never tasted nothing like that – so good! And be plenty of goats and sheep. They make best cheese and meat and share with everybody – the workers, the family and friends, and good, good wine they make.

Some people who remember tell me I look like my father. But I don't know. I can't remember him face. I feel him a little, but not how him face looks like. I wish to remember, but no pictures. Everything be destroyed by fire in wartime. Our house be burning three times.

My father and my brother Ljubo be killed together in 1942 – I only be little boy. My father be forty or something little more and Ljubo be twenty-one – he be my favourite brother because he caring for me very much – he playing with me. He have wife and baby who be one. His son not have daddy anymore – just like me.

My second oldest brother be fourteen – they try kill him too. They shoot him two times. He pretending to be dead – he lying very still. Other bodies fall on top of him. He move and boom – they blow off some of him leg with dummy bullet. After war, he go to Italy and have fourteen operations.

My mother and other women from our village be crying very much, 'Please don't kill my husband, my sons'. I hide in my mother's long skirt because I be scared very much.

Men with guns they say, 'We will kill you too if you not stop crying'. But how we stop? We crying and crying – everybody from our village is crying.

Commander he come – he tell men with guns not to shoot the women and children. Commander only want to kill the men. We not be killed only because he said no kill us.

The men from our village crying too, 'Please don't kill us! We be innocent! We not fighters! We villagers! We do nothing wrong!' But they not listen to him. They take the men… and young men too, the teenagers, behind the houses and shoot them – dead.

When men with guns go away, I pick up bullets from ground. The bullets have blood on them and I put the bullets in my pocket like a toy – to play with. I never have real toy in all my life; only some rocks in sock for ball. I crying when I pick up the bullets."

⚜

Before the executions, some said it was safest to hide in the caves and others said it was safest to stay at home, in the village.

Dad's family often hid amongst the shrubs and in caves throughout the mountainous terrain. They slept in caves every night during the war and huddled together in fear. In the winter it was very cold and damp, yet they never dared to light a fire, as they were too afraid of being found out.

During the war it was my Baba's prime duty to protect the family house, possessions and livestock from looting, while my Dida and uncles hid. She feared most the militia men with fire.

Her house was set alight and wine barrels were smashed, flooding the cellar with thousands of litres of wine. She was beaten badly with a rifle butt when she refused to disclose the whereabouts of her husband and sons. In reprisal, Mara was pushed into her burning house, yet escaped.

On the day of the executions, the villagers decided not to go into hiding but to remain in their homes as they had been informed it was safe to do so. However, they were terribly deceived.

Dad's duty during the war was to care for animals. He took goats and sheep to pasture every day, where he often encountered snipers who shot at him from higher ground. As he ran the bullets hit the rocks around him. There was an old stable in the vineyard in which he took cover. There he hid for many hours until he felt quite certain the snipers had forgotten about him. Then he gathered his flock in a great hurry to get home. He was always afraid.

Droplets of hope came in the way of cans of Spam falling from the sky. English warplanes dropped the most splendid Spam my dad has ever tasted. American warplanes dropped biscuits and powdered eggs. Dad thanks Mr Churchill and Mr Truman for saving his life.

It was sobering hearing the details of the dreadful circumstances leading to the splintering of our family. Dad continued to recount events from his life to me over a number of visits to his home; in kind, his near-death had spurred a review and assessment of his life. I was in a sense his guide, asking him questions along the way. The sharing was therapeutic and gave us both perspective and resolved a chasm in communication that had existed between us. It also made it possible for me to move on from the mental gymnastics of trying to decipher our family dysfunction and pain.

It is fair to say, my dad has more lives than a cat. Over the next six months, our family held more last suppers in dad's honour than I care to mention and yet he recovered from each life-threatening operation he endured. During this time he experienced numerous visitations in the night from spirits. He was frightened to see an illuminated woman standing in his bedroom doorway or in his room, gently watching over him. However my spiritual experiences gave me the confidence to assure him that he was not going crazy, rather beginning to transition between this world and the next. More than likely the illuminated woman was his guardian angel caring for his spiritual wellbeing.

"I *never* believe, if I not see her myself," he whispered to me one day, in case Uncle Roger should hear through the fence and think he was mad.

It was a remarkable admittance by my once non-believing father.

"It's ok, dad," I said, "I believe you." My reassurance appeared to settle him. He returned to sweeping the path and to his own private thoughts.

The situation made me think back to my dad's uncle, who when alive and aged, also reported seeing an illuminated woman of spirit in his house. My dad didn't believe it at the time but now that he was having his own spiritual experience, it was difficult for him to deny its reality.

When dad's uncle was dying in the hospital, we went to visit him. I was particularly fond of him because of his kind and gentle nature. He was the first of my dad's line to immigrate to Australia. And he was also the closest living link I had to my grandfather who had been executed. We sat close to his bedside and he was barely audible, but when he slightly moved his head toward dad, I heard him tell him that dad's deceased father Ivan had been to visit him. He had appeared to his dying brother at his bedside the day before. My dad politely said nothing in reply, which I knew meant that he didn't believe a word of what his uncle was saying. Rather he thought the old man's mind was rapidly deteriorating as he was approaching death.

His uncle then told my dad that he'd also been back to visit his homeland (Croatia) to see the house where he'd been born – which was the same house my dad was born in. My dad politely remained silent.

"I *really* was there," his uncle vowed.

I understood exactly what my great-uncle was attempting to share with us. He'd had a visitation from his brother in spirit, who was assisting his transition from this life to the next. He'd also had an out-of-body experience and his spirit had returned to the place of his birth because it was particularly meaningful to him – he may even have experienced a life review.

"I believe you," I assured my great-uncle, taking his hand. "I really believe you. I know these things are possible." This gesture seemed to settle him and he began to sleep. We never heard him speak again. A few days later, he died aged ninety-six.

Following my dad's disclosures, I was able to I let go of the powerful attachment I once had to the tragedy he suffered as a boy. I felt my dad had found some kind of peace with the outcome of his life and that the spirits of my ancestors had transitioned to a loving living realm that was as real if not more real than the physical world. I felt my family's grief finally dislodge from me and it ushered in new life and optimism. I soon became pregnant with our first child and there were many more experiences to come that further strengthened my understanding of the indestructibility and versatility of the spirit and the potential that exists in all of us for personal and intergenerational healing.

SIXTEEN
DIVINE ILLUMINATIONS

ONE OVERRIDING PERCEPTION I have from my observations during out-of-body experiences, visions and acts of inspired creativity is that reality is a complex and methodical arrangement of holograms. It is as if existence itself is made up of infinite reflections of light.

When experiencing states of consciousness that exist at higher frequencies to the physical plane, reality becomes increasingly abstract. For instance, spiritual beings can appear as solid as people do in physical form or as light bodies (illuminated spiritual replicas of the physical form) that can quite fluidly then transform into symbols, shapes, colours and white light.

The divine light by its nature expresses itself in countless ways, including the following, from my lived experience.

White Horse

I awoke to a magnificent white horse galloping towards me at an almighty pace. It was incredibly powerful, awesome in fact. It thundered yet it was silent. It was the most beautiful beast I had ever seen, made entirely of light. It was as if I was watching a silent motion picture illuminated entirely by a Godly power source. The horse was very lifelike, yet it possessed the unmistakable quality of spiritual illumination, so that it appeared to also shimmer from within.

As it galloped, exuding strength and liberty, I observed it from the same vantage point – I was always just right in front of it. The horse galloped towards me but it never passed me. I couldn't see myself but I was aware of myself. I was Linda just as she is – every bit of me alert and present in the experience. The horse was aware of me too. It was overjoyed. I was its beloved. I could never have imagined a creature loving me so completely.

The horse was awakened, that is, it was supremely conscious – not simply some exotic other-worldly beauty, though it was beautiful beyond words.

Extending away from the horse's billowing mane were rays of rainbow fluttering in the wind like carnival ribbons. The exceptional vibrancy of these colours was a divine expression of love, celebrating my homecoming.

I then entered a state of divine rapture and became one with the horse. God was the horse and I became God. I was pure white light. There was The Light and nothing else. I was utterly at peace, boundless, in infinite celebration of life eternal.

Multiple Lives

I awoke to another silent motion picture illuminated by a Godly power source. It took up my entire view. I knew instinctively that I needed to pay close attention. As I did, it was as if a giant torch was being flicked on and off, and every time the light came on I saw the face of a different man.

I was shown countless larger-than-life-sized faces of men. The faces were three-dimensional and made of light. They flashed before me at an almighty pace. I observed them with extraordinary focus. I knew I had been all these men. My soul had experienced a physical life as each of them.

It was made apparent to me that I had been a man of every race upon the Earth. I felt no particular affection or disaffection for any of the men I had once been. I observed them without attachment. I knew that what mattered to my soul was not the personality of each man, but the experiences he had lived. My current lifetime was the result of all the experiences I had ever lived. Of this I am absolutely certain.

Light Body

I awoke to see my husband hovering over me, quite literally, in mid-air. He was a metre away from me, facing me, so that his eyes were staring down right into mine. Rob was made entirely of white light. In image his light body was a complete replica of his physical body. It looked magnificent and magical. As he was asleep naked under the bedclothes, his light body was also completely naked. I was so shocked to see him there in the air staring at me, that I screamed out loud. Rob suddenly awoke back in his body.

"What just happened," he said, stunned, lying next to me.

"You… you just freaked me out!" I stammered.

No-Mind

My mum, as always, presented an elegant table – a rich coffee aroma filled the dining room. There were vases filled with roses from the garden. Generous plates of cakes, slices, chocolates, nuts, and dried and fresh fruits were arranged in a precise manner on a crisp, stark white table cloth with cloth napkins. It was early afternoon, following lunch. Mum, Mary, her husband and I had congregated about the table for a coffee-cup reading. My dad and

Rob were watching football on the television in the lounge room, disinterested in our entertainment.

I picked up my brother-in-law's coffee cup. It was a beautifully coloured pearly cup that looked like it belonged to European royalty. These delicate cups, from the old country, are the one thing I hope my mum will leave me, some day. I looked inquisitively at the 'mud' inside the cup. The dirty appearance of the cup with dark granules against a light, pearled backdrop creates intricate pictures and symbols that I can sometimes decipher and give intuitive meaning to. Upon this occasion, there was the distinct image of a white horse at the bottom of the cup that Dave had just drunk Turkish coffee from. It was so clearly a white horse and I was stunned at its perfection.

"Look at this beautiful white horse in Dave's cup," I showed each of them. They all agreed that it was very detailed. It made me think of the vision I'd had, of the divine white horse that caused me to enter the heavenly state.

I suddenly felt the need to close my eyes. As I did, a surge of energy rose in me. It buzzed in me like a moderate current of electricity. I felt heat rising up my legs and the muscles of my thighs began to quiver. The heat moved through my torso and up into my head. My entire face and my eyelids began to twitch. My breathing changed, becoming very slow and deliberate. I breathed this way without intending to, it just felt natural to do so. I felt myself withdrawing from everyone and everything. My hearing diminished so that sounds appeared off in the distance.

"Linda, what's happening," I heard my mum say to me with a tone of concern.

"Mum, ssshhhh leave her," Mary hushed.

I felt very far away from them and I couldn't feel my body anymore, at all. My sense of identity dissolved and I felt on the verge of nothingness, yet there was something to the nothingness and this something was a sense of *being*-ness.

I existed but I wasn't anyone or anything in particular. I wasn't a personality. I wasn't a mind even. I was *no-mind*. I had no-thought. I was peace, quietude and contentment. I was the void rather than the fullness of God. I was the dark rather than the light of God. I understood then that God was both the dark and the light, the in and the out, the up and the down. There was no evil present in the darkness, rather what I was experiencing was the vast emptiness of God. It was a deep, dark tranquillity, something that would exist at the bottom of the deepest ocean.

The whisper of me that was attached to having an identity began to freak out. My mind wanted to exist so very, very much. It simply couldn't stand the thought of not existing. It began to slap and to flap around in the waters of no-mind, frantically trying to turn around so it could swim back to the shores of self-reflection and self-deception. It was afraid of irrelevance. It was afraid of death. It was afraid of having nothing to concern itself with. My mind increasingly generated a focus that willed me back into my physical body. I opened my eyes to see three concerned onlookers staring back at me.

"Are you ok Linda?" my mum asked, afraid.

"Yes," I said.

"What just happened?" Mary asked.

I looked at her. "I don't know," I said. I just didn't quite know how to explain The Dark of God.

Blessed Mother

I was six months pregnant with our first child. I went to bed and fell asleep on my left side, with a pillow between my legs to support my belly. Sometime later I awoke in the heavenly realm, out-of-body.

I stood, looking out at a beautiful clear pale-blue sky to the east, as the sun rises, when suddenly there appeared a veiled figure that was very large in the sky. Though I viewed her from behind, I fell to my knees in instant recognition.

I was in the presence of an exceptional force and I was utterly overwhelmed by it. The figure turned to face me – *it was the Blessed Mother*. The spiritual energy she emitted was so potent that it caused me to weep spontaneously, and my breathing to become deep and long. She then assumed a lifelike stature and moved in close to me. Had I wanted to stand up before her, I simply couldn't have – it was impossible to do so. I felt absolutely rooted to the ground.

The Blessed Mother stood before me, as I knelt in awe. She was draped in soft, luminous, pastel blue-pink cloth that looked alive and moved like liquid mercury. Her pink veil cascaded down from her head to the ground over a flowing blue garment. I continued to kneel and to weep spontaneously before her. I couldn't speak but I could gaze upon her face, which was but a whisper away from mine. She took my hands in her hands and held them for the longest time.

A warm, pulsating energy passed from her hands into my hands. She radiated supreme spiritual love and her power, which was extreme, caressed and healed every crevice of my being. It rippled throughout with the greatest feelings of pleasure and wellbeing, unimaginable.

"I have come to offer you spiritual strength," is all she said to me, purposely, with transference of thought, while looking directly into my eyes. It was as if her eyes were transmitting her communication – I sensed energy being emitted from her eyes. Her demeanour was serious, though I felt her complete acceptance of me.

She was not particularly beautiful or outstanding in her features and certainly she did not resemble the delicate statues dedicated to her in places of worship. She looked like an ordinary woman of forty years, and there was something endearing about this to me. She was not dark skinned or light skinned, but she had dark features. Her eyes, brows and the rim of her hairline were dark.

In this instance, the power of Spirit did not manifest as a geometric shape, a light or a horse but as a woman – as the divine feminine. God was also a woman and the source of limitless, living light. She was the feminine powerhouse of life. She was creation and sexuality. The Divine Mother and I became one. I entered into a state of ecstatic spiritual perfection – I was home again.

☙

I had the great privilege of experiencing the Blessed Mother, when Oliver was in gestation. However, it took a couple of years for my mind to comprehend what had happened to us, and more years still to comprehend it at greater depth.

There are many levels to integrating mystical experiences. These kinds of experiences seem to ripple – the effects are far-reaching and reverberating.

My initial consideration quite naturally was why did the Blessed Mother visit me? Why did she give me and perhaps my unborn child the gift of her healing light? During the time before this particular experience, I didn't think about her at all. I did as a child, rather fleetingly.

After I'd matured I didn't really believe in her as a supernatural entity – a super being. Yes, most likely the spiritually enlightened man named Jesus had a mother named Mary or Miriam… but a virgin mother with exceptional other-worldly powers – unlikely. I had thought of her as yet another embellished religious figure built up on folklore, and an unattainable role model for women the world over to feel the lesser by.

I now know without any doubt that the Blessed Mother exists for real. However she exists beyond the dogma of religious constraints. My experience of her was as the sacred feminine. I felt an abundance of sexual energy emanating from her and so I still very much doubt the virginal attribute she's gained historically. She allowed me to feel her sexual power completely, which on the grandest scale was a celebration of the creation of all of life.

This dynamic 'creation' power resides in each and every life form that has the potential to create life or to assist in the process of creating and nurturing life.

Eight years prior to my encounter with the Blessed Mother, I'd been to Medjagoria in Bosnia-Herzegovina, with my parents and my aunt (my mum's youngest sister).

During regional conflict in the 1990s, my aunt's front door received a sniper's bullet and I'm sure she did her fair share of praying at the time. In addition to the stresses of war, her husband developed cancer and they had three children to care for. The up side of this tale is that she and her family survived their enormous life challenges and have gone on to prosper.

When we visited my aunt's home, she wanted to take us to the holy site of Medjagoria, which was nearby, famously known for the miraculous sightings of the Blessed Virgin Mary by six Catholic children in 1981.

At Medjagoria, my dad and I joked about the lucrative trade of tacky plastic trinkets and postcards imaged with the Blessed Mother. Further fuelled by the fact that none of us had experienced an apparition of the Blessed Mother on that day.

I did, however, say a silent prayer at the holy site. *Blessed Mother, please appear to me.*

I looked up at the clear blue sky above the simple wooden cross mounted in the stones and witnessed nothing out of the ordinary, apart from a crowd of devout worshippers. I went away and rather quickly forget about the Blessed Mother and my prayer to her. That is, of course, until she did appear to me some years later. I was then once again left with the strongest impression, that prayers *are* heard in heaven. And communicating with heaven and its spirited inhabitants is something that is possible for all.

SEVENTEEN
MEDIUM

THE LOCAL SHOP had sold out of the Saturday paper so my husband came home with the Sunday paper instead. He put it down in front of me on the dining table where I was eating lunch. I flicked through it between mouthfuls of food. It was full of tabloid headings and bad news, which is why we rarely bought it.

My eyes then glanced over an ad about a psychic medium, who would be giving a demonstration of his unique ability in the city the following Saturday evening. It would also be his first book launch. I knew nothing of him but felt drawn to attend the event, so I flagged it. I knew very little about how a professional medium engaged with spirits in an audience setting, but my personal experiences with Pete's mum and Aunty May gave me some insight into after-death communication, so my curiosity was aroused.

I continued flicking through the paper and came across yet another ad for a psychic medium, this time a lady, also scheduled to give a demonstration the following week, on a Wednesday evening, near the city in Subiaco. I was surprised to see the two ads in a mainstream newspaper. I flagged this ad too. I had no aspirations to connect with any of my deceased ancestors but I was fascinated to see other people connecting with theirs.

I went along alone to the Wednesday-night demonstration though it was cold and wet out. Our firstborn, Oliver, was fourteen months old and it was the first time I'd been out at night, during his life.

When I arrived, I entered an old community hall with a small crowd of people. We sat on plastic chairs before a slightly elevated stage. The hall had wooden floorboards and high ceilings. About eighty women, some with their men, chattered in pairs and appeared rather upbeat, but there were some solemn faces amongst them. I wondered who in spirit they were hoping to connect with.

After a few minutes, a middle-aged English lady came out on stage and introduced herself as the medium. I could sense she was nervous because she worked a little too hard at being funny, which was a little offputting. She was probably hoping to God that the dead would show up.

The medium briefly explained how she worked and then began her spirit communication. It took me by complete surprise, when the first connection she made for the evening was with a spirit named Delilah.

"Does anybody know a Delilah?" asked the medium. "I have Delilah with me and I feel like it's someone over here." She gestured to the middle of the audience.

There were two ladies from the audience who knew a Delilah that had passed and I was one of them. My hand shot up, straight in the air, but the medium wasn't keen on me because I was off to the left side of the hall. The other lady who knew a Delilah was sitting in the middle of the audience.

The medium gave details about spirit Delilah's family that I couldn't agree with or deny, because I just didn't know for sure. The other lady who wanted the spirit to be her Delilah was also not sure.

"I have an 'S' name, close to her, does that mean anything to you?" she asked the other lady.

"No," she said reluctantly.

"I'm hearing a 'C' name too?"

"It does to me," I called out. "Stewart and Craig are my Delilah's children."

The medium looked at me briskly, preferring to stay with the other lady instead.

"There's a Margaret connected to this Delilah," the medium said to her.

"Possibly," said the other woman.

"I think it's my Delilah's mother's name," I interjected.

"Are you planning a trip to New Zealand?" the medium asked the other lady.

"No," she said.

"I am," I spoke up again. "My husband and I have just been talking about visiting New Zealand."

"Do you get bad headaches?" the medium asked me, finally, with her hand on the back of her head.

"Yes," I said, "that's me." For the first time in my life I was pleased to be the one with the bad headaches.

"You need to sort that out," she said.

Well, that's insightful, any idea how? But a remedy wasn't forthcoming.

"This Delilah is for you then," the medium said to me – and I smiled. I felt like I'd won a prize.

"Who's Fay?" she asked me.

I looked at the medium blankly. I had no idea who Fay was. The medium looked to the previous lady and she shook her head too. Then she scanned the audience.

"Anyone know a Fay?" But there was only silence.

"I'm hearing Fay," she said. Nobody raised their hand.

"Come on people," she said, "there is a Fay in spirit wanting to communicate with someone here." The audience was silent. It was getting a little bit awkward.

At this point, two of the more solemn looking people in the audience got up and walked out of the hall.

"Bye," the medium said to them as they left.

"Why is no one admitting to knowing Fay...?" the medium continued with a pained smile. "She won't go away... I'm hearing the 'ay' sound so clearly," she said, "Fay, Jaye, Gaye, Kay...?"

"Oh! It's me!" I spluttered. "Sorry, that's Delilah's other name but you weren't saying it quite right – it is *May* – not *Fay*."

The medium paused to look at me for a split second with a 'you're a big twit' expression on her face and I felt a bit silly.

"Often I only hear part of a name," she explained. "I'm now hearing an 'R' name, Rog(er), Roy or Rob," she said without hesitation.

"Wow – spot on – to all those names," I exclaimed, "Roger is her husband, Roy is my dad (his 'Aussie' name) and Rob is my husband."

"That's Delilah's way of saying it's her, she's *really* here with you," said the medium, and then she paused. "She has nice energy."

"Yes, she does," I agreed.

"Who's got the issues with their heart?" the medium asked me.

"My dad," I confirmed.

"Ok... I can feel her pulling away now," she said. "Delilah wants you to know that she's ok. That she made it over."

"Thanks," I said. I knew this already but it was further confirmation.

"She says 'Hi'," said the medium, in parting.

"Hi," I said back.

✧

A few nights later I went to see the psychic medium, Anthony Grzelka, at the Alexander State Library in Northbridge. Once again I went alone and my intention was merely to observe the proceedings.

As I squeezed passed a few people to get to my seat, I could feel the anticipation in the theatrette mounting, as time fast approached for the seminar and book launch to begin. There were hundreds of people present and an equal show of men and women. I thought, *This man must be pretty good at what he does, to attract a crowd like this.* The seating arrangement was such that the stage was at ground level and the seats tiered upwards toward the ceiling. The theatrette was darkened and a spotlight went on.

When Anthony walked out on stage there was an outburst of enthusiastic applause. Then something quite unexpected happened. I felt a sudden surge of energy pass through me that I can only liken to a powerful sense of destiny. It was a rare and unmistakable feeling. I sensed this man, was pertinent to my life story.

It was therefore, with even greater interest that I watched the medium from Eaton (Bunbury) known as Australia's Ghost Whisperer, as he made numerous connections over two hours without pause, between the people in his audience and their dearly departed.

Anthony possessed a remarkable sensitivity, making spiritual connections effortlessly and with incredible accuracy. Even those husbands who had been coerced along by their wives to the event were visibly affected. I did not receive a reading – regardless, it was a powerful and moving experience for everyone.

A few days following this, I was at home with my son. I had sat Oliver in his highchair for lunch when he pointed at a small white envelope on the kitchen bench. He was very intent on the envelope, so I handed it to him.

Oliver opened the envelope and removed from it the entry ticket to Anthony's seminar, the one I had just been to see. On the ticket was a picture of the medium and he paused to look at it, holding it firmly in his little hands. He then looked at me directly, right into my eyes with a piercing stare and pointed his finger at me, his arm outstretched. I thought, *That's a bit odd.*

He studied the picture for a second time and then he pointed his finger at me in the same manner as he did before. *How unusual.*

When he repeated this act for a third time and with the same intensity, I felt the back of my neck prickle and flush with heat.

"Are you trying to tell mummy something?" I asked my toddler, a little cautiously, at which instant he turned around in his highchair and very deliberately pointed at a hand-painted Nepalese mandala, hanging on the wall. The gesture rendered me speechless as he was pointing at a powerful spiritual symbol – one that meant a great deal to me. Oliver had never before shown any interest in this art work. The mandala was a gift from Mary who had trekked in the Himalayas and to me it was *my* God symbol.

What exactly was my son trying to convey to me? Perhaps, that like Anthony, I would one day come to help others connect with heaven?

I suddenly felt my son's timeless nature. He was not his fourteen-month self, he was something greater and this something greater was communicating with me. Oliver turned back to face me and put the ticket down, satisfied that his message had been delivered – then began to eat his lunch.

Months later I attended another of Anthony's public seminars, but this time I went with my sister.

"I'm getting the feeling to go up here," Anthony said, pointing to our row in the audience. "I have two suicides."

Mary took the microphone.

"Yes, our cousins – this is my sister," she gestured to me.

"They have transitioned and they have the support of family, in spirit," he said. "They are all here together. There are a lot of them."

We nodded our heads.

"Who died on the motorbike?" he asked.

"My sister's godmother's son," Mary said, a little anxiously.

"What's the significance with the 'A' name closely connected to him?"

"His brother's name begins with that letter," she said, breathlessly.

"He wishes his brother a happy birthday – it must be about now. Perhaps you can pass that on."

The medium paused, thoughtfully.

"There's a lot of tragedy in your family," he furrowed his brow.

We agreed by nodding – we were both feeling very emotional.

"I have your grandfather here now," he said. "I feel that it's your dad's dad and he's showing me that in life he wasn't able to be there for your dad... like somehow he was prevented from being there."

At the mention of our Dida, I felt like I was going to faint. I felt like my heart was going to burst and I could sense that Mary was feeling the same way.

"Wait... was he a prisoner of war," Anthony asked, "because he is showing me his wrist and I am seeing numbers, like the kind you would see marked on a person in a concentration camp during the Second World War?"

"You're on the right track, Anthony," Mary explained. "He wasn't a prisoner of war, but he was executed during the Second World War – our father was there also – he was a little boy when it happened."

"I know this must be difficult to hear," Anthony hesitated, "do you want me to go on?"

"Yes, please do," Mary and I spoke in unison, eager to hear more about our paternal grandfather.

"I feel he was shot in his chest. I can actually feel his lungs filling up..." the medium said. "He couldn't believe this was the way his life would end – he wasn't ready to go."

We both felt upset hearing this and it was rather excruciating feeling hundreds of eyes boring into us from the audience. But to hear him speak of the man at the centre of our family tragedy, as if he was there, before us, was incredibly cathartic.

"He's in a really good place now," Anthony assured us. "He's happy – he's really close to your dad, in spirit, and he has been throughout your dad's life."

To hear this pleased us immensely. I felt like crying mostly at hearing that he was still connected to our dad.

※

Again months later when I attended a private session with the same talented medium my paternal grandfather, Dida Ivan, made his presence known to me. He was quite the conversationalist, along with other deceased relatives who relayed specifics to Anthony that he simply couldn't have guessed. Even his pronunciation of Croatian names was remarkably accurate.

"Who's Delilah?" Anthony then asked me.

"My neighbour," I said.

"Passed?" he asked.

"Yes," I said.

"This lady is very connected to you," Anthony said. "She supported you from quite a young age."

"Yes, she did," I agreed.

"She kind of adopted you," he said, "took you under her wing."

"She did – my parent's both worked a lot," I explained, "and she looked after me."

"She's a gentle soul," Anthony said. "The kind you'd like to have for a grandmother."

"Yes, she would have made a wonderful grandmother," I told him.

"Who's Margaret, connected to Delilah?" he asked.

"I think it's her mum," I said.

"She says 'Hello to Margaret'," he said.

"Ok," I nodded.

"I've got to tell you," Anthony said seriously, "it's very rare to see it of someone you've known in life and who then passes; but she helps you with your spiritual work."

"I'm so glad you've said that," I enthused, "because I feel her with me strongly at times and then sometimes I wonder if I'm just imagining it."

"No, you're not imagining it," he assured me. "You're both very connected spiritually. She's *really* aware of you."

"I feel bad that I didn't visit her when she was sick, before she died," I confessed. "I feel I could have supported her more, knowing what I do about the afterlife."

"I can feel from her," Anthony said certainly, "that she harbours no bad feelings about any of that – she is totally ok with it."

"Really?"

"Yes, really."

I felt relieved to hear it.

"She's a very sweet lady," he said – and I agreed, wholeheartedly.

EIGHTEEN
POWER OF THOUGHT

BY MY THIRTIES, I'd become accustomed to experiencing the extraordinary but the frequency of my out-of-body experiences had diminished. Since becoming a mother at thirty-two, my sleep routine was awfully interrupted by our son's nightly feeding and waking. And I felt I didn't have the time or energy to devote to my spiritual practices, like mindfulness, meditation, chanting and painting.

Despite our many efforts it wasn't anything Rob and I did that finally resulted in Oliver sleeping through the night – it just happened. And with improved sleeping, I was able to recall my out-of-body adventures with greater clarity once again.

It was night when a familiar ringing sensation woke me and I began to rise from my body. It was the sound of worlds tearing apart – a shrieking, a shedding – so very startling but I was *not* afraid. For the first time, I wasn't reluctant to leave my body, even a tiny bit. Something had changed in me. I felt surrendered and at peace. I was free, truly free, in all aspects of myself including my mind.

Vibrations pulsed and flowed, sweeping me upward on translucent waves. I went with it, easily and I felt pleased with myself that I was not afraid anymore. I had grown an enormous trust in the mystery awaiting me.

I sensed Malachi with me, the captain of my ship, the great overseer – always present for my expeditions in and out of the body. The same energy I sense at my left shoulder during the day. The voice I hear speaking to me in the quietude and out of thin air – my greater self and most dedicated companion.

My spirit separated from my form like heat rising from pavement. I was an effortless, temperate breeze like that which carries the hawks high into the tallest pine trees near our house. I was awake, aware, clear minded and I was myself, as I knew myself to be – Linda, wife, mother, daughter, sister, friend… and yet I was more. I was supernatural.

I sensed my body in bed, lulled yet magnificent still, a complex piece of machinery made of flesh, blood, bones, yet temporary. But I am not temporary. I of spirit – I am indestructible life. My mind was completely accepting of this truth, when previously it had struggled to let go of the temporary reality, of form, of the material, even with all the experiences it had ever had.

As I floated in spirit, I thought, *Be upright* and I was – I began to move. I passed a small mirror on the wall and fleetingly glimpsed my illumination. I then moved through a wall. *How did I do that?* I wondered. I felt utterly amazed to have passed through a 'solid' object. *It's as easy as moving through the air.*

I moved along the hallway passing Oliver's bedroom. I glanced into his room and sensed he was quietly asleep in his crib, in the darkness. I felt great love for our little boy.

The house was dimly lit by electronic gadgets and the street lights seeping through the curtains – all appeared as it should have. I moved along another hallway that led to the kitchen. There I paused behind the counter where we prepare meals and I looked onto the adjoining dining room. It was exactly as we had left it, before going to bed.

From the bedroom to the kitchen I simply went with the flow but once in the kitchen I began to focus my mind deliberately. I thought, *If I focus my thoughts on passing through the (dining room) window, it should happen.* I did so and immediately my movement accelerated and I passed straight through the window. Out and up into the night's sky I flew like a bird.

I felt in control of my out-of-body experience for the first time. I was able to do this entirely with my thoughts that were malleable like putty. My thoughts caused things to happen.

Passing through the window was easily done. It was like moving through the wall and through the air. There wasn't any resistance.

I soared over the tall trees at the park across the road from our house. Up, up into the night's sky I flew, where I paused to observe a kaleidoscopic sky. It was breathtakingly beautiful, an ocean of black, sparkling with diamond-like stars.

I was eager to explore my extraordinary abilities and began to focus my thoughts again. *I want to visit my girlfriend Tessa, who I haven't seen in a long time.*

I concentrated on her intently and my movement accelerated at such a speed, I was like a rocket ship taking off, only faster and less encumbered. Almost immediately, I was at Tessa's bedside where I observed two of her lying side by side. It was an amazing sight to behold and I was awestruck.

Her body was asleep in bed but her light body was magnificently illuminated like a crystallised beacon of magic, floating next to the bed in the air, in the sleeping posture. There were two Tessas lying side by side, one made of flesh and the other made of light, identical in their features.

My sudden arrival on the scene startled Tessa made of light in the same way as if I'd unexpectedly roused her in body from deep sleep. It surprised me that a light body could be startled, so easily. She was every bit the Tessa I knew her to be, only supernatural, like me.

"Hi Tessa," I said to she made of light, greeting her as I would do in everyday life.

"Oh, you scared me," she said.

Her light body sat upright, still hovering in the air. She was then pleased to see me, as I was her. I too was identifiable to her.

"Try to remember that I came to visit you, like this," I said to her, referring to our rather extraordinary night-time rendezvous before parting.

Next I thought I'd visit an American friend I hadn't seen for many years, not since I was an exchange student. I held the focus of him strongly and my movement accelerated. I had the sense of speed like a gale blowing but without any feeling of environment.

My movement began to slow of its own accord and I could see that I was descending upon a congested metropolis. There were many, many tall buildings – I was approaching New York City. It was either dawn or dusk.

Then all of a sudden I was in a void of pitch darkness, blacker than black and I sensed my friend there too – there my memory of the experience ceases. I woke in the morning, back in my body. I called my friend Tessa on the telephone to ask her if she remembered my visit in the night.

"I've been really sick with the flu," she said. "I don't remember a thing from last night."

I felt a little disappointed – the out-of-body adventure remained vividly with me.

On yet another memorable night my spirit took flight for outer space. My inspired paintings had shown me that my spirit had voyaged the cosmos before, but this was the first occasion I felt I could direct my experience. I passed by celestial bodies, marvelling at the sights. *I'm out-of-body again and I'm travelling through the universe. This is remarkable!*

I want to visit Mary in England, was my next thought. My sister had moved there with her young family for work and I was missing them. I held my focus of her in mind. As I did, I picked up an awesome speed, flying through pitch darkness. The pace slowed and the scene became vividly colourful as I approached land upon the Earth.

I had the same view as someone would when parachuting. I could see far and wide, and there was a lot of beautiful green countryside. It was a bright and sunny day. I slowly descended upon a house and watched its rooftop near – and there my memory of the experience ceases.

As I had experienced firsthand the immediate effects of focusing my thoughts, this creative power then became very real to me. I began to apply it with earnest to my daily life and magic ensued.

I had been creating vision boards for longer than it had been popular to do so, but now I took to the task with enhanced gusto and conviction.

My love for vision boards first started back in the seventh grade when my teacher, Mrs Crawford, got our class to imagine what our future might look like. I thought it was a lot of fun cutting out pictures from magazines, to represent my future life, and sticking them on a poster.

My future then looked like an episode of *Dynasty*, but since then my focus has shifted from acquiring material acquisitions and accolades to fostering a meaningful home life, my personal wellbeing, creativity, spirituality and community.

Following the two out-of-body experiences I directed with my thoughts, I decided to make myself a fresh vision board. I had new ideas about what I'd like to experience next in my life and so I created an exceptional future in pictures and words on a sizeable piece of ply wood. My board was covered in the books I'd like to write, the art works I'd like to paint, the people I'd like to meet, the places I'd like to go, the house I'd like to live in, the relationships I'd like to foster, the health and vitality I'd like to activate, the mind I'd like to grow and the world I'd like to live in.

Perhaps I'm thinking too big, I thought, looking over the kaleidoscope of inspiring images.

"Why not?" said a voice.

I cut out a picture of a fifty-dollar note and stuck it on the board, to generate future financial prosperity in my life. *I need a picture of myself, to make it more personal.*

I opened a drawer in my wardrobe and rummaged through it, looking for a photo of myself. Then 'by chance' I came across an envelope. I opened it and saw it was a Christmas card. I pulled the card out to see who it was from, and two fifty-dollar notes fell out into my lap. The card was from my parents, from almost a year ago and I had entirely forgotten about it. *Wow, that's rather immediate. Maybe I should stick up more than a fifty-dollar note on my board.*

"Why not?" said a voice. So I did. In thick black texta I wrote YNOT across my vision board and it became my new mantra. Every time I had a doubt in mind, I said to myself, *why not*, as a way of inspiring a change of thought.

A few days later, I took Oliver to the community nurse for his check-up. When we returned to our car following the appointment, I placed him in his car seat and strapped him securely in. As I shut his door, I noticed another car drive in. The entire car park was empty but this car pulled up in the bay right next to us. *How strange, I would not have done that.* I walked behind my car to get to the driver's side and caught a glimpse of the vehicle's registration plate. In big, bold black letters it read, *YNOT. Wow! Some coincidence!* The woman in the car stepped out. I could see her baby within. She was obviously here for an appointment with the same community nurse.

"What's the significance of your number plate?" I asked her.

"It's my husband's name spelt backwards," she said, "Tony."

A few days later, I walked down the road from our house to playgroup, at the local kindergarten, pushing Oliver in his pram. As we approached the gate to go in, a vehicle pulled up close by, parking right in front of the gate – I couldn't miss seeing it. No other car had parked on this side of the road – only this one. The vehicle's registration plate read, in big, bold, black letters, *YNOT 72*. A woman stepped out of the vehicle. We were relative newcomers to playgroup so I didn't know her or her baby yet.

"What's the significance of your number plate?" I asked her.

"It my husband's name spelt backwards," she said, "and the 72 is his birth year. He tried getting just plain YNOT but it was already taken."

No kidding, I just met the wife of the man who took it. What are the chances of that?

A few days later, Oliver and I went to our local charity shop to see if we could find a treasure to buy and as we approached the front door, I noticed a car parked right in front of it – I couldn't miss seeing it. Its registration plate in big, bold, black letters read, YMMOT. No doubt Tommy or his wife was somewhere in the shop.

Is someone trying to tell me something, like perhaps I should invest time and purpose into my thoughts? I'd definitely received the blaring message (as is often the case when things come in threes): *if you believe, all things are possible.*

Oliver has an uncanny ability for manifesting his heart's desire. Also, he can be very intuitive. Very young children are prone to this, as they haven't yet been stifled by limiting thought patterns.

Early on in his life, I encouraged Oliver to speak to his angels. This comes into play at odd moments, like when we were travelling in the car from his grandparents' house. I overheard him in the back, whispering, "Please angels send me *six*, *big* Cat machines, right *now*."

Geez, why does he have to start off by asking for massive things like that? Why not a packet of lollies or a small toy? "Your angels might be a bit busy at the moment, darling," I said, trying to lessen the inevitable disappointment to come.

We then turned a corner to take the long road home, following the train line. It was only then, to my amazement and relief that we saw stretched out before us, exactly *six*, *big*, bright yellow Cat machines parked on the verge.

"Look mummy, there they are. My angels *did* hear me! See!" he said, delighted.

"You've got some powerful friends," I said. "Don't forget to thank them."

"Thanks angels!" he chirped.

I thought, *This is yet another reminder that I should never underestimate the power of thought or the power in asking heaven's helpers for assistance.*

"Next I'll ask them for a scooter, mummy," Oliver chirped.

"I'm sure it'll turn up soon," I said.

Sure enough, one day soon after on the way to playgroup, there was a broken scooter thrown into the bushes that my boy noticed. We took it home for daddy repairs. By the weekend, the scooter was operational and being enjoyed by our son. He thought it was the finest scooter in the world.

"Angels, I'd like a bike next," he said.

"You already have enough," I told him, "enjoy your scooter for now."

But at the next verge council pick up there was a bike left out on the verge, which he promptly claimed, happily riding it home. Oliver thought the old, rusty thing was the best looking bike ever – he thought his angel friends were pretty cool too. And that piece of throw-out has taught our son how to ride.

It's my turn, I thought. We required a loungechair, so I pictured a blue loungechair in my mind's eye, to match in with the blue armchair we already had.

A couple of months later I felt a powerful urge to visit the charity shop. When I turned up, there was a near-to-new lounge chair that had arrived in store that morning – someone's throw-out in the same fabric, colour and design as the armchair we already owned, but at a fraction of the cost. Now it's the most comfortable seat in our house.

A TV please, and five were given to us without us asking anyone. A dog please… and the kind we had imagined in mind was given to us, well trained. An excellent community for our children… and Oliver was granted enrolment at a most desirable school, though we live outside of its boundaries; affordable family getaways… and our dear friends regularly welcome us to stay at their enchanting country farm. There can be no denying that focused thoughts make things happen – sometimes in magical ways.

NINETEEN
HALLUCINATIONS & DELUSIONS

OLIVER AND I visited the local library every third week when he was a little boy and it was just the two of us with his daddy at work. He loved to go there and to look for children's books to borrow. He also loved to jump on the beanbags and to swivel on the chairs.

It was during one of these occasions when he was two-and-a-half that I came across a book titled, *Transformed by the Light*, by Melvin Morse MD with Paul Perry, about near-death experiences (NDEs) and how people have been fundamentally changed by encountering The Light. When I saw the book on the shelf I thought, *Well, I've been transformed by The Light* and so it aroused my interest to take a closer look.

Up until then I knew little about the phenomenon and the characteristics and after-effects associated with it. I'd never come close to dying, so I had never in all the years I'd been reading spiritual and self-help themed books thought to examine the NDE. I didn't consider the dying phenomenon relevant to me – *how very mistaken I was!*

Reading Dr Morse's book later at home, I learnt about the traits that characterise a NDE. These were my experiences too.

I returned to our local library, my son in tow, ever eager for another visit there. I borrowed the classic NDE book, mentioned in the first book I'd read on the subject – *Life After Life* by Raymond Moody MD, PhD, a psychiatrist. It was published in 1975 – the year following my birth.

Reading this book at home, I made note again of all that I shared in common with the phenomenon of NDEs and there was a lot. Then I returned to the library and took out more books on the subject and learnt that different experts had different models by which they characterised the phenomenon. Again, these were my experiences too.

It truly baffled me that it had taken me so many years to join the dots together, to see the bigger picture, and that no one in my life had noticed the parallels too. Here what I had lived was described by a number of reputable researchers.

I felt jubilant! There were people in the world who had been through something similar, who would simply 'get it', who were equally impacted as I by the spectacular scenes and beings of heaven – and it brought me immediate relief to know this.

Enthused, I then rang a local university to find out if any scholars were conducting research into NDEs or if there were any other kind of consciousness study underway. There was not, however, I came into contact with a professor of psychiatry who was interested in meeting with me and hearing more about my experiences. I felt validated and, in preparation for my meeting with him, I compiled a thorough overview of my experiences to date. It turned out to be one of the best things I ever did, because it was the blueprint for this book. Also, it put an end to the congestion in my mind.

The professor met me at the front door of the research centre where he worked in the city. It was a few floors up from ground level and

I had to announce myself through a device in the wall. He peered through a glass panel and then the door clicked – I was let in.

My initial thought of him was – what an unusual man. He was little in stature and I towered over him. He was very serious and quiet in manner, making no attempts at friendliness, which rather surprised me. I wondered how anyone received a healing from such a sombre psychiatrist. As we walked together down a very long corridor, he said absolutely nothing to me, not a peep. I however offered him (and the walls) sporadic chirps of friendliness in an attempt to break the awkward silence. The awkwardness however remained well intact.

We entered his congested office which, though light and airy, was crammed full with papers, journals and books. I looked across the room and out the window, at a perfect blue sky. *He's odd but rather clever,* I thought. I suspected that every book on the shelves that reached for the ceiling had either been read or written by him.

The professor sat at his desk that also was drowning in paperwork and motioned for me to take a seat opposite him, which I did. I looked at him across the desk, anticipating his cue so we could begin our discussion.

"I specialise in the field of schizophrenia," he alerted me.

What's that got to do with me? I wondered briefly.

"Can you describe for me your out-of-body experience?" he stated matter of factly.

"Well, there's more than one," I explained.

"Start with the first one then," he said.

For close to an hour we discussed only the first out-of-body experience I ever had, at age sixteen. Within the first few minutes I had the sense that the professor didn't believe in the authenticity of my experience. Yes, I might well have had the experience of feeling separate to my body and I believed it was real; but, no, it was actually not real but a trick of the mind.

"This is a neurological condition known as autoscopy," he said.

"Auto-what?" I queried.

"Autoscopy... you saw an image of yourself in external space, but you were viewing it from your physical body," he explained, as he quickly drew me a diagram that represented what he was speaking of. "You saw yourself as if you were being reflected in a mirror."

"Umm no... that's not how I saw myself," I tried to explain.

I told him that during my first out-of-body experience, I didn't see myself lying in bed at all and that in other out-of-body experiences I consciously took little pleasure in viewing my flesh body, it rather frightened me, though I always sensed where it was – I had viewed it once.

I also mentioned having seen my girlfriend's flesh body and her light body, lying side-by-side and that of my husband's – but the professor all but rolled his eyeballs at me in obvious disbelief. It was disappointing, to say the least.

"What then do you make of these experiences?" I finally asked him.

"They were most likely hallucinations caused by an overstimulated left temporal lobe," he said.

"Ok," I said, taking this approach, "but what *power* do you think was actually behind the stimulating?"

He paused to look at me rather intently – was it an unreasonable question?

"Many of my patients have hallucinations," he continued, "and they seem very real to them."

"What, ones of exceptional love and acceptance – that cause profound healing to occur in their lives?" I asked.

He replied by offering me something of a smirk that he then quickly overrode with no expression at all. I didn't think that the hallucinations people with schizophrenia had were particularly uplifting or insightful.

"Professor, do you believe I'm schizophrenic?" I asked him plainly.

"No," he said. "You are not."

I didn't think I was – but I simply wondered why he had asked me in. Our discussion was going nowhere and was of no real benefit to either one of us, so I thanked the professor for his time and let myself out.

Unfortunately, my meeting with the professor had planted a seed of doubt in my mind that festered there, in the background, for months. Initially I wasn't aware of it, but I started feeling unsettled in a way I hadn't for many years. *What if the best experiences of my life have merely been like mirages on a desert plain,* my mind mulled?

I felt there was not one person in my life with who I could discuss this. I no longer attended Claire's meditation group, as motherhood was taking up all of my time. And, even so, she wouldn't encourage talk about such things. I could see her point. I was somewhat preoccupied with my spiritual experiences; after all, flying through space without an astronaut's suit or a rocketship is not an everyday occurrence. However, I felt that my other-world experiences had enhanced my happiness, and that others could benefit from them too. Still, I needed help integrating them into my life. But from whom could I get this kind of assistance?

Then one day, I woke up with a good measure of courage and made an appointment to see my GP, thinking I should get another perspective on the matter. I was thirty-four, pregnant with our second child and I didn't want this becoming a bigger issue for me in the months ahead. I hoped she could refer me to a counsellor, someone with an open mind. When I saw my doctor, I mentioned divine lights and out-of-body experiences.

"It's always good to have these things looked at, just to make sure…" she said caringly. "I know a very good psychiatrist who'll be able to assist you."

Well, this will be interesting, if nothing else – after all, perhaps I am mad.

At my first appointment, the psychiatrist, a friendly man in his mid-life, made a long list of the unusual occurrences I'd experienced throughout my life.

"What do you make of it?" I asked him, at the conclusion of the hour together.

"These hallucinations *are* concerning to me," he said.

There's that word again, yet it wasn't entirely unexpected – he was an enthusiast of the professor I'd seen.

"Hallucinations?" I queried.

"Perhaps you've been having epileptic seizures while you've been sleeping," he explained.

"What about when I haven't been sleeping?" I asked.

"The mind can conjure up all kinds of things," he said.

"Like delusions?" I queried.

"Yes," he said.

Well, maybe I am crazy, after all – and all the hope in the world drained out of my veins.

I'd never considered it a real possibility before. Yes, I'd been concerned with people's perceptions of me, thinking that I was an odd ball, but I didn't actually believe I was mad. Perhaps that's what a person with a mental health illness does – they think they're perfectly sane when actually they're not. I imagined a world with no divine power, no soul, no heaven, no afterlife, no magic, no hope, and it was *hell.*

When I got home I rang my sister. "Do you think I'm crazy?" I asked her.

"How do you mean?" Mary said.

"With all the spiritual experiences I've had, do you think I've actually lost the plot?" I wondered.

"No, you're not crazy, Linda," she said, "… annoying sometimes, but not nuts." *Well, that's reassuring because I've got no delusions in that regard – I'm annoying quite regularly.*

At my second appointment, I asked the psychiatrist, "Can you disprove God's existence to me?"

"No, I can't," he said. "Can you prove God's existence to me?"

"No, I can't," I said. "You can only know God for yourself… through your own experience."

That afterthought was something of an earth-shattering revelation to me, in the most unlikely of circumstances.

"The hallucinations," he went on, "are only really of concern if they're interfering with your life."

"My spiritual experiences have deeply affected me," I admitted, "but they haven't *interfered* with my life, not in a negative sense – in fact they've been the best experiences of my life."

He appeared surprised to hear me say this, and it was true. I'd had many wonderful times in life, especially as a mother, but nothing beats an encounter with God/Spirit.

"At some stage we'll have a scan done of your brain," he said.

"Oh, I've already had one of those," I explained. "I saw a top neurologist because I was having bad migraines and the results came back all normal. No tumour. No bits missing. Apparently my brain is in full working order."

This second appointment was the last occasion I saw the psychiatrist. It turned out to be a turning point in my life – when it all came together in me. I feel I truly awakened on that day, in the spiritual sense. I suddenly grew an enormous, unwavering faith in my own spirituality. It was the merging of all my life experiences into one expansive reality – which is the perspective from which I now live my life entirely.

As I drove home from the psychiatrist's office, I recalled Claire saying to me once before, "On the spiritual path, love, when you are at the point of questioning your own sanity, you are on the verge of great clarity."

I finally understood what she meant by this. I had gained enormous clarity. I realised then that a person can have all the mystical experiences in the world, but without faith in one's own experiences, it is of little value.

I felt a great peace settle over me and I have never again questioned the authenticity of my experiences, of God/Spirit, heaven and the soul, or of my intrinsic connection to all of these – *or my sanity.*

The need I once had, for the support and understanding of others entirely left me – I simply let go. For me, it became enough to be able to share my knowing with my children – the truth of eternal life, divine love and the connectedness of all things.

This major shift of perspective drastically reduced the blistering migraines I had been experiencing for ten years. Our second son was at fourteen weeks gestation and I felt buoyant again – there was so much of life and love to be looking forward to.

TWENTY
PREMONITIONS

I WATCHED MY MUM as she arranged wilting flowers into a bouquet. I woke with a start, my heart racing in the darkness. Someone mum knows will die soon… I knew.

The following day I told her of my premonition and a week later my mum's friends died instantly in a head-on collision with a semi-trailer while holidaying in northern Western Australia. They were husband and wife and had an award-winning garden into which they put a lot of their time and effort.

During her walks around the neighbourhood, mum often stopped at the front of their house to give compliments on how lovely their garden was looking with all its pretty blooms. Following their deaths, no one attended to the garden and it wilted. The house was later sold with the garden in disrepair.

… My cousin Deanna was driving a car and I sat next to her in the passenger seat. Deanna turned to look at me.

"I'm pregnant with a boy," she said and I woke with a start.

The following day I rang my parents.

"Last night, in a 'dream', Deanna told me some happy news – she's expecting her first baby."

A week later, I went to my parent's home for dinner and my father opened the front door.

"You're a witch!" he exclaimed jokingly. "We just hear on phone, Deanna pregnant!"

"I bet you a hundred bucks it's a boy," I smiled. "Perhaps you'll start believing dad?" He laughed – Deanna delivered a boy.

… I'd lost touch with friends from university who moved overseas and lived in California.

"We're getting divorced," they told me, together. I woke with a start, in the early hours.

A year later, I discovered they had divorced at the time of my vision.

… My girlfriend, Rhonda, opened her mouth wide and pointed to her teeth.

"My teeth and gums are really sore, right here," she said, pointing to her top left molars, then – "I'm sick with the same cancer my mum died from and I have four months to live."

I woke with a start, my heart pounding.

The next day, I called Rhonda on the phone. I hadn't spoken to her for many months.

"Are your teeth and gums hurting in the top left part of your mouth?" I asked her.

There was silence at the other end of the line.

"How did you know *that* Linda?" she said, astounded.

I felt dread hit the pit of my stomach. *Is Rhonda going to die?*

"I dreamt it last night," I said, regrettably.

"My gums and teeth *are* really sore and right where you said!" she exclaimed.

"You need to get that checked out," I said, "but not just with a dentist. Go see a doctor about it too," I encouraged, "… it's just a feeling I have."

We talked about our kids and made other chitchat.

"While I think of it," I mentioned casually, "make sure you have regular check-ups with your doctor, too, particularly since your mum had cancer."

"Yes, you're right, I should," Rhonda agreed.

My friend remains in good health but her sister was diagnosed with breast cancer four months following my vision. Her sister went on to have a mastectomy and is now doing much better.

I was six months pregnant with our second son, Daniel, when I woke in the early hours. This baby was particularly active and big. I felt him move for the first time at fifteen weeks. My obstetrician called him my bonnie baby.

It wasn't my bonnie baby who woke me up from my luscious sleep, rather it was a high frequency buzzing sound I could hear all about me. It was different to the piercing shrill that usually accompanied one of my out-of-body experiences. Rather, it was an enormous humming sound – like the sound of a million bees.

A great spiritual energy was descending upon me, and I knew to pay close attention to all that was about to transpire. The power in our bedroom felt immense, intense and rapid. There was almost too much power present for my mind to bear, but I was not afraid. All my senses were fully aroused and on the highest reception, anticipating the supernatural insight to come. I felt a familiar presence was with me again, faceless, formless, genderless yet there and everywhere, as always, supportive – *Malachi*.

As I focused on the darkness a light began to grow. It grew so strong in brightness that I was transfixed by its magnificence.

I knew then, without a shadow of doubt, that the light before me was an angel.

I had never seen an angel before – that I could remember. Now that I was in the presence of one of these glorious beings of light, I thought, *This is not what I imagined an angel would look like.* It didn't have wings or feathers or a celestial robe, or extraordinary features like cascading blonde locks or shimmering eyes; rather it was an intense luminosity that radiated gentle yet powerful love.

The angel was a band of sheer, perfect light; yet, it was also a complex arrangement of energy. The light that was the angel was somehow different to the light that I had previously experienced as God/Spirit – it felt different. Though it was made of the light of God, it was also distinctively an angel.

As I marvelled at this splendid being that glistened with exceptional beauty, more angels appeared before me. Then more angels appeared still, until my entire view was a tranquil sea of transcendent luminosity. These divine energies were indescribably the most exquisite lights, shining as do the most perfect crystals in the most perfect sunlight.

I felt the angels' generosity of spirit and their unconditional love for me pulsate outwards and into my being, like heartbeats in unison throughout eternity. Peace permeated every fissure of my being.

I thought, *Angels are real, they truly exist!*

"We are everywhere, supporting all of humanity," I felt their communication within me. "You are not alone."

Then the tranquil scene changed suddenly to one of peril. I observed people running in fright through a rusty, dusty doom. They were bewildered and their hearts ached and cried out in dismay, "Oh God, why is this happening to me?" The scene was very real, having a three-dimensional quality to it. I was there amidst them, in the chaos, though detached in a way, like a ghost.

I then observed myself as a girl, with Malachi at my side

– a tall, bearded, dark-haired man, robed. We were bound at our wrists. Malachi shone a light through the rusty, dusty doom and together we passed through it.

The scene then changed swiftly again and, in quick procession, I observed six women who I had been in other lifetimes. Each woman sat in a similar pose and looked very much alive. As I observed these esteemed women in the prime of their life, I heard each of their names spoken out loud by a strong feminine voice. Their names all sounded melodic, majestic and ancient, like nothing I'd ever heard before in my present lifetime. I understood each of these women was spiritually awakened, and that the knowledge they gained from those lifetimes would come to help others in this lifetime.

Swiftly, the scene changed again and I was in outer space, quite literally. It was very dark and quiet in outer space. I felt every bit myself yet I was also much more of myself – I was expanded. I possessed a far greater awareness of reality.

It felt very natural to be in outer space. I looked upon the Earth from a distance. It appeared perfectly round and remarkably peaceful. The Earth glowed like a radiant gem, a planet of rare beauty. From this vantage point, it was obvious to me that the Earth is a living entity with spiritual purpose. It provides the conditions for the giving and receiving of love in form. If everyone could see the Earth like this, their desire would be to protect it from any harm. There would also be a feeling of humble gratitude – for the abundance the Earth provides.

I looked upon the distinctly shaped continent of Africa and had a sense of what would transpire next, however, I felt detached from the outcome. A rock hurtled passed me, quietly, yet as large as it was, an impact with the Earth would be anything but quiet. From my position in outer space, the rock appeared about one third the size of Africa and it was on course for a collision with the heart of the continent. I didn't observe it hitting the Earth and there was hope yet for a better conclusion.

I heard a communication boom from the angels, "Fighting amongst humans must stop!"

This powerful message reverberated throughout my being and the universe simultaneously. *Our survival depends on a new way of being.*

These magnificent beings of peace spoke with one voice, urging all of humanity to foster a spirit of friendship and gratitude for the Earth which provides, so generously, life in myriad forms.

I understood, with all my heart that nothing can snuff out the blazing light of the soul, not even the bleak scene shown to me. The future *is* malleable and our collective choices determine our shared global experiences.

The high-frequency humming all about me dissipated like a breeze out the window. I felt the awesome energy pulling away from me like the ocean rolling back on itself.

I heard my husband breathing methodically as he slept next to me in bed, unperturbed. I looked at the alarm clock – 3:15 am. I stared at the wardrobes in the darkness while absorbing into memory this truly phenomenal event.

The angels, their parting audible words lingering in my mind and almost too fantastic to fathom, "Humans will come to live on Mars." I couldn't sleep and so began my day with an enormous sense of urgency.

༄

I was heavily pregnant with Daniel, when an Anglican priest came to visit me at our home. Rob had seen an article about the former police-chaplain in the local paper and encouraged me to call him. The priest was researching the near-death experience and the out-of-body experience phenomena for a book he was writing. I hoped that I could be of some assistance to him.

When Father Barry May walked through our front door I liked him instantly – he was tall in stature and friendly; he exuded presence. I poured him a glass of orange juice and we sat at the dining table. We then talked easily for two hours.

The priests I had known previously where rather rehearsed but Father Barry was not. Perhaps it had something to do with the fact that he was a dad and a grandpa and could relate in everyday terms, or it may have just been his character. He listened carefully, respectfully, and it was obvious from his responses that my experiences moved him.

The symbolism of 'a man of God' sitting at my table, with my belly brimming with new life, was not lost on me. I no longer sought validation for my world-view and yet here I was receiving ample support.

I described to Father Barry the various out-of-body experiences I'd had, my encounters with The Light, the Blessed Mother and angels. It was quite a different conversation to the one I'd had with the Catholic priest, some years earlier, following my first encounter with The Light.

"Hearing of your experiences will give people hope," he said, thoughtfully. "People need hope in life."

"I don't really know how to go about sharing my experiences with people," I said, "I mean, I've tried…"

"Write a book," he said. "Don't give me anything for my book. Keep these experiences for your own book instead. There's enough here for an entire book."

"But who will believe me, Father?" I asked.

"Don't try proving anything to anyone," he said. "Just tell it like it is – the rest is up to them."

Epilogue

D URING MY SECOND pregnancy at eight months gestation, I was diagnosed with swine flu and I felt the closest I ever have to dying. I felt so sick I believe I should have been hospitalised, but my doctor simply told me to go home and to start counting foetal movements.

I returned home and promptly burst into tears, fearing for our baby's life. I lay in bed, passing in and out of consciousness as the illness worsened.

The following afternoon, I began experiencing stomach cramps and though I called out for help, Rob was outside speaking with our neighbour and didn't hear me. I was so worried I was about to lose our unborn child that I began praying to the Blessed Mother for the first time since her visitation – it was three and a half years on from then.

As I prayed with all my heart, asking her to protect my baby, I immediately felt warmth ripple through my body. It brought me a sense of peace and wellbeing, and I suddenly had the powerful feeling that my baby was going to be ok.

Immediately following my prayer, the phone rang. I reached out for it, as it was next to where I lay and a girlfriend whom I hadn't spoken to for months was on the line. She wasn't aware of my illness but had felt a sudden urge to call me.

"I just felt so strongly that I should call you," Margie said, "and say that everything is going to be ok with your baby."

The timing of her call was uncanny and I felt then, as I do now, that she'd been inspired to call me.

My mum, during the illness, was a powerhouse of love and support – as she so often has been throughout my life. She took the very best care of me and my children. She arrived at our house with cooked meals, she cleaned and she entertained our little boy Oliver for days, wanting to help, when others preferred to stay away.

It took me three weeks to recover from this illness. Daniel was born soon after, healthy and happy. In fact, he left Subiaco's Saint John of God Hospital heavier than his birth weight. The nurses weighed him and then again, just to be sure.

The greatest gift of love to come from this difficult circumstance, which I attribute to the power of encountering the Blessed Mother, was a deep forgiveness and acceptance of the past. I was able to recognise more clearly than I ever had before (though there had been numerous opportunities throughout the years to do so) the extraordinary love my mum has for me.

I was able to let go of previous disappointments and expectations, in a way I hadn't thought possible – to feel deep gratitude for the very first relationship of my life.

I dropped Oliver off at kindergarten and was deciding how Daniel and I would spend the morning before his day sleep. Behind the kindergarten was a playground that we often frequented in the afternoon, and on the right side of the kindergarten was an open playing-field that led on to a tennis club.

On this particular day my toddler was intent on roaming the playing field. It was a grassed area with trees bordering its periphery and there was no one about but the two of us. I chased after him and he squealed with delight – then he took off with some determination for the tennis club. I called him back to me but he wouldn't return.

I caught up to Daniel and we walked through the tennis club car park and stood together before a closed gate with a small courtyard on the other side of it. Through the gate we could see a small playground where my son wanted to play. I scanned the area and could see no one about, so I let him through the gate. *No harm done*, I thought.

We had never before ventured so far from the kindergarten on foot. I didn't know there was a little playground here. Once we'd entered the courtyard, I saw a gardener tidying around the tennis courts and he didn't take any notice of us, so I relaxed a little more.

While Daniel played on the climbing apparatus and slide, I thought about the next chapter for my book, which I would begin writing later that day when he was sleeping. It was to be about my experiences with the spirit of Aunty May. Right then I called on her to fill me with inspiration so I could give the best kind of expression to her story of spiritual survival.

Then a sign in a window caught my eye, so I went up to it – it gave the details of a playgroup operating from one of the little rooms on the outer of the tennis club. I peered through the window to see what kinds of toys were available there for toddlers.

I heard my son shuffling about near me on the pavement, to which I had turned my back. Then a man's voice broke in.

"Hello, little fella," he said to Daniel.

I turned around to see who was there, expecting to be told to move along. And of all the people in the world, there stood Stewie, smiling at me, from behind a pair of fashionable sunglasses. His mum had died some six years earlier and I hadn't seen him since the funeral.

"Stewie, is that you?" I stared, startled.

"Linda... hello!" he chuckled.

Indeed it was. *Blimey!* I was flabbergasted. *Man, she's quick.* I was almost expecting Aunty May to materialise before us.

I introduced Stewie to my youngest son, whom has often reminded me of Stewie as a baby. I then discovered that he managed the tennis courts. So for months our paths were close to crossing, but never had, until the day arrived that I was to write Aunty May's story – what impeccable timing.

I knew Aunty May had synchronised this meaningful encounter. It gave me the opportunity to tell Stewie that I was writing a book that would honour the spirit of his mother. He then told me that that day just so happened to be his parent's fortieth wedding anniversary.

And he was also able to resolve a lingering curiosity in me – *who exactly was Margaret?* It was not Aunty May's mother after all – she was Ada.

"Margaret is dad's girlfriend," said Stewie with a warm smile – Uncle Roger had found love again.

In preparing this book for publication, I reviewed a number of books to see how these were formatted. One of these books was *Heaven is for Real*, by Todd Burpo with Lynn Vincent. In the centre of Burpo's book are a number of photographs – one photograph is of a painting by child prodigy and visionary Akiane Kramarik, titled, 'Prince of Peace'.

Kramarik's 'Prince of Peace' is a representation of Jesus.

When I first viewed this spectacular painting by Kramarik, which she created at the age of eight, it took my breath away, because of its remarkable resemblance to Malachi – *My angel, My messenger (God's angel, God's messenger)*, who finally appeared to me in my angelic vision and who led me out of the rusty, dusty doom.

Acknowledgements

I HAVE MANY wonderful people to thank, most sincerely, for assisting me in this book's development and publication. Firstly, my beautiful, effervescent children who have kept me grounded throughout. I hope one day my story will be very meaningful to them.

My darling husband Rob, the most patient of men. It is not easy being married to an 'experiencer' or a writer or an artist. But he is always kindhearted. I am very fortunate and ever grateful for the space, time and understanding he has allowed me in writing this book, and getting it out into the world.

I wish to acknowledge my parents, in a big way, for their generosities – for emigrating to Australia, where I feel I have the freedom to speak my truth; for caring for my children so I could write; for sharing their life stories with my readers. Also, to my mum for teaching me early in life, that books have the power to change lives, for the better.

Sometimes people enter our lives for the shortest time yet inspire great movement. Father Barry May of Embleton was one such individual. Though our exchange was brief, towards the close of 2009, his encouragement set into motion the writing of this book. I am grateful he visited me at my home, and for his kindness.

Thanks to Jennifer Marr, cofounder of the pioneering Western Australian human potential bookstore, the Inspiration Factory, for sharing her vast knowledge of books, branding and the publishing industry with me.

Michael Grosso, an accomplished philosopher and author – was a connection I made in 2012 through a magazine article he'd written, and the first interaction I had with a respected consciousness researcher. Technology, fortunately, makes the world a much smaller place and Michael's support for my project, all the way from Charlottesville, Virginia, USA, spurred me on in my endeavours – for which I am most grateful.

I wish to acknowledge Penny Sartori, a pioneering NDE researcher and author from Swansea, Wales, UK, and her marked contribution to this book. Penny wrote its foreword just a month before giving birth to her little miracle, her son! I feel very appreciative of her generous support.

The following individuals, all leaders in their fields, have helped in moving my book forward – I thank them very much for their advice and for reviewing my manuscript: Yolaine Stout, former president of the International Association for Near-Death Studies (IANDS) and founder/president of the American Center for Spiritually Transformative Experiences (ACISTE); Jody Long, NDE researcher, author, and webmaster of the Near-Death Experience Research Foundation (NDERF); Pim van Lommel, cardiologist, pioneering NDE researcher and author; Nancy Clark, IANDS Columbus, Ohio facilitator, NDE researcher and author; Phillip Laird, IANDS Perth, Western Australian facilitator and author; Robert Bruce, astral projection authoritive and author; Anthony Grzelka, Australia's leading medium and author; Frith Luton, Jungian psychotherapist and author; and Barbara Parks, paranormal investigator and author.

Special thanks to my editor, Frith Luton, and to Maryann Agnello, for improving my writing at different stages of the manuscript's development – and to Rob and my sister Mary for assisting me with proofreading. Also, to the team at Damonza for creating a fantastic book cover and internal design.

I wish to acknowledge the gifted astrologer Chris Lambert who many years ago foresaw a future for me in books and publishing. His words have long inspired me.

There are many other people who have been an inspiration to my writing over the last few years: my family, friends, neighbours, strangers, authors and online community – thank you to you all – the list is long. Our dog Harry has sat at my feet as I have tapped away at the keyboard – thanks for being a furry comfort.

A final big-hearted thank you to my dear, irreplaceable, iridescent, companions of light, *'the delightful ones'*, who have made their presences known to me, inspired my words, as well as the emotion behind my words, and have collectively moved me forward along this epic, challenging, therapeautic and joyous writer's journey.

About the Author

Linda Cull was born in Australia of Croatian immigrant parents. She is a visionary artist and has worked in administrative and research roles for State and Federal Members of Parliament. She studied politics at universities in the United States and Australia, and was an intern for the Human Rights sub-Committee in the Australian Federal Parliament.

As a teenager, Linda was diagnosed with idiopathic scoliosis, which caused her pain and contributed to her culture of grief. She was further impacted by the war trauma that pervaded her family life – her father was a child during the Second World War and witnessed atrocities. Her recovery from depression and intergenerational grief began spectacularly, at the age of sixteen, when a series of transcendent experiences set her free.

Linda is living proof of the hope for renewal and meaning that can come out of adversity through fostering a personal relationship with Spirit within. She currently lives in Perth, Western Australia with her husband, children and dog.

Visit the author online at **www.lindacull.com**

www.ingramcontent.com/pod-product-compliance
Lightning Source LLC
Chambersburg PA
CBHW021125300426
44113CB00006B/301